Bette Davis

BETTE DAVIS

a celebration by Alexander Walker

arch by The Kobal Collection

Little, Brown and Company
Boston   Toronto

For Maria Teresa del Rosario Licaros
– who knows the odds, too

Library of Congress Catalog Card No 85-82201

First American Edition

Printed in Great Britain

The following illustrations appear by the kind
permission of: Museum of Modern Art: 22, 24, 26
(TL, B) 27, 53 (B), 54 (C, T), 58 (CL), 85 (BR), 128, 136
(BL), 172 (R, L), Filmography: 3, 9; Paul Popper: 23,
25, 54 (TL), 102 (L), 109, 129 (B), 132, 136 (T), 145 (T),
147 (T); National Film Archive: 28, 32, Filmography 2;
BBC Hulton Picture Library: 29 (L), 53 (T), 54 (R); Rex
Features: 64, 169 (T), 173, 174 (L);
AP/Wide World Photos: 79; Photosource: 151; Channel
5 NY: 174 (R); NBC: 175 (L); The Press Association:
175 (R)

CONTENTS

THREE ENCOUNTERS

Work: *Elstree Studios, England, 1967*

IT WAS LIKE AN UNROBING AFTER A CORONATION. The star sat on the film stage in a toe-length gown the colour of the green Caribbean with enough gold embroidery on it to sink a Spanish galleon. And handling it with the ease of familiar regalia, she stripped off her make-up.

Off came a false eye-lash like a shark's fin. Off came a curiously shaped eye-patch that masked the other supposedly sightless eyeball in her film *The Anniversary*. Off came a skull-fitting 'bald' wig with an odd babyish fringe to it that deftly suggested the childish wilfulness of the domineering matriarch she was playing. 'And now,' quipped Bette Davis to the attendant wardrobe girl, 'just let me unscrew my leg and you can take it, too.'

Gothic jests are in order. 'Mother Goddam', as she accepts people calling her, is back in London in the sort of role that carries no risk of her saying, as she did at the end of her last British film *The Nanny*, 'I was so sweet, I practically nauseated myself.'

At fifty-nine, Bette Davis still radiates the combustible energy of a thirty-six-year career that has worked on her the way that heat and pressure work on carbon to make a diamond and given her the power to cut her mark into a role, a script, a film. This is her seventy-eighth.

Stand still when you step on the film set and, as they teach you on safari, let the big game do the approaching. She scents you out. For Hollywood has bred in Bette Davis an almost psychic awareness of people. You understand all the better why that memorable line in *All About Eve*, 'Fasten your seat-belts. It's going to be a bumpy night,' is uttered by her with a matchless sense of someone sniffing blood on the wind.

She has already had one director fired from the film. Although she approves of the replacement, she is not going to surrender possession of a role that's rare in every sense – as juicy and oversized as a steak cut off the flank of one of the steeds ridden by the Four Horsemen of the Apocalypse. This is Mrs Taggart, a rich English matron who stops at nothing to keep three adult sons under her thumb. 'The film is a black comedy,' she says, 'the title refers to my wedding anniversary, though I *insist* on celebrating it ten years *after* my husband's death – all the better to keep the family together.

'It's a role, I think, that gives a mother back the initiative in the Oedipus complex. When I hug the youngest of my sons who has had the *nerve* to get engaged, I plant a kiss on him that's more than motherly and then fling at his fiancee a challenging "*Follow that!*"' Her eye-patch is there to prick the family's conscience by reminding them that one of them nearly blinded mother in a childhood prank. 'It's called a demi-domino – the name of the style is actually 'Moon Flower Petal'. Somewhat rosy-eyed in these circumstances, don't you think? I tracked it down in a little New York shop which sells them custom made. It's called 'For Thine Eye Alone'. She chuckles at her shameless enjoyment.

Did her green-and-gold housecoat come custom-made, too? 'Not at all. It *looks* as if it were designed 'For the Matron with a Viper in her Bosom,' doesn't it? Actually it was a Christmas present. At last I've found a use for it.

'The important thing is never vanish into your make-up. I do one or two TV shows a year, mainly to let people see me as *myself*. Your public want to know seventy-five per cent what to expect from you every time. You've got to decide how different you can afford to be. That's the trick.'

I hazarded a remark that it was odd that she once wanted to play Alice in Wonderland. She gave me the look out of *The Little Foxes* – the one that considers whether to leave my heart drops out of reach.

'But Alice was like *me*! An odd-looking kid,

I had these big eyes, this long neck – Holly-wood had seen *nobody* like me before. The trouble was in the early days they didn't know how to cast me. They tried glamourizing me and it left producers in a state of shock when they saw the screen tests. You see, if they were out to make a *star* of you, they couldn't afford to let you play disagreeable parts – *that*'s what held me back.'

Yet she looks more indulgently now on the contract system that used to tie a star to one master for years: she herself stayed at Warner Bros for eighteen years. 'It had this advantage. If one film flopped, you simply began another. The public got time to know you. The contract system gave actors a kind of negative reassurance that today's young independent players don't have when they stake all on one or two films. The children today do too little work. And what's gone out of today's youngsters is the old *yearning* to play a role that's so good

you'd kill to get it.' William Wyler is the man she credits with the making of her career. 'Wil-lie was no ice-cream director – he didn't care if you *melted* away, so long as he got his shot. After thirty takes for a scene in *Jezebel*, I said, 'Willy, for the sake of my *sanity* show me the first take, then one in the middle, and the one you're going to use.' I couldn't believe my *eyes* when I saw myself getting better in each one. After that, Willy yelled, "Marrrrvellous!" no matter *what* I did, till I told him to shut up and go back the way it was. I swear to you, I fought with my bosses only when I knew that they knew I was in the right.'

No one should be surprised, either, she insists, that however big the rows, she was always back at work within a day or a week.

The eyes flash. 'But then I'd learnt what it takes to survive in Hollywood. Number one: the strength of an ox. And number two: a short memory for who did what to you.'

11

Rest: *Connaught Hotel, London, 1978*

BETTE DAVIS PAUSED AND THOUGHT AND THEN
had to acknowledge that, yes, *Death on the Nile*
probably was the first whodunnit she had been
in. 'Absolutely staggering,' Perhaps it is
because we don't think of her other films as
whodunnits, I suggested: it is usually taken for
granted that she is the one who dun it (whatever it may be). What was that line of Margo
Channing's? As I'm trying to recall it, she sup-
plies it: 'Write me one about a nice normal
woman who shoots her husband.' For a few
seconds, the penthouse suite of her London
hotel resounds with the familiar gratifying
witch's howl of laughter.

Miss Davis has had a hard-working year, but
she hasn't had to 'nibble the scenery' once to
get her way. She looks rested: indeed she looks
at rest. She wears an amber-beige dress with
a tie belt, high-waisted and ruched. There is
gold gleaming at her wrists. What looks like
jade glows in the folds of her dress, beside a
locket the size of a small pear. Inside it, two
small grandsons' portraits, much admired for
the family hint of iron in the jawline. Nothing
here to connect with the kind of Hollywood
glamour that used to trail mink wraps around
like old ponchos.

Yet she hasn't lost one Hollywood attitude
I observed when we met over ten years ago. She
keeps her distance, settling herself all of ten feet
away across the cushiony and coffee-tabled
suite with that psychic awareness of people that
stardom breeds in those who have discovered
from bitter experience that human relationships are dangerous things and the only sure
thing is one's own dedication.

It has been non-stop the past year. She has
been changing employers and latitudes with the
exhilarating abruptness of someone very much
'in demand'. First there was Disney, who
catches all stars sooner or later (usually later).
Then it was into a witchcraft shocker based on

12

Tom Tryon's *Harvest Home*. And *then*, with only three days to pack the lighter things from I. Magnin, it was straight off to scorching Cairo for seven weeks of *Death on the Nile* in which she plays an autocratic American matron. 'It is *not*,' she asserts, holding one of her innumerable cigarettes like an antenna, 'a part that needs acting. The only one of us in the film who really *acts* is Peter Ustinov, who plays Hercule Poirot. Mine's the sort of role that requires a "pitch" to it, rather than a performance. When I first read Tony Schaffer's screenplay, I hoped – Oh God, how I hoped! – that I was the one who dun it. But I'm part of, well . . . a larger ambiguity.'

The waiter enters with tea and she expertly stage-manages the room, as if it were a film set, making it 'work' for her so that I do the pouring and sugaring – a captive interviewer, as she intended.

As night falls over Park Lane, she rises to pull down each blind just the right distance, as if the script demanded it.

She's been reading Agatha Christie's posthumously published autobiography and has found it a painful experience. Not because of the book's contents: simply because it involves an act of looking back, which contradicts everything her mother, 'Ruthie', ever taught her. 'Looking back is *ghastly*. You have to be so hard on yourself in order to be able to speak a few home truths about other people. I wrote my life story ten years ago. But I always said I'd need to wait till at least ten more people had died before I could really tell *the truth*. Actually, people tell the world too much nowadays. Autobiography is no longer about confession – it's about bragging. The great thing I admire about Agatha Christie? Why, her power to deceive.'

Bette Davis understands the nature of power like no other contemporary star. Kissinger could have taken a few lessons at her knee. I reminded her that the last time we met she had just got her director dismissed. 'But I *assure* you' – her voice, now that there is a challenge in the vicinity, assumes the emphatic pitch that has grown with the years – 'that I am *much* more affable than rumour allows. I have convictions, yes. I've done wilful things, yes: many times in my life. But stubborn, *I am not!* I may engage in a trial of strength with a director – but directors *ought* to value those who contribute ideas. The director not to be tolerated is the one with no ideas of his own.'

Mastery is her ultimate satisfaction. Of all the eighty-odd roles she has played, I asked, what is her favourite? She didn't hesitate for a moment. 'I could play Elizabeth Tudor every year at the drop of a hat – or a head.' Again the howl of laughter. Lost chances? 'They never really are lost – there's always hope. In 1948, when I was at Warners, they announced my next picture would be *Ethan Frome*, the Edith Wharton classic, set in my own New England, with me as the servant girl Mattie who falls in love with Ethan. Because all the moral laws of the time are against them, they try to commit suicide. It ends with Ethan's wife, Zenobia, having to look after a crippled twosome.' Her eyes gleamed with lost regret. 'For some reason Warners shelved it – I'd wanted Gary Cooper for Ethan – Mildred Natwick was actually tested for Zenobia. *What waste!* Now, fortunately, the book's out of copyright, so they're not saddled with the cumulative expenses of options. As I see it today, Henry Fonda would be Ethan, Liv Ullmann would be Mattie and I'd have to be Zenobia. Well, maybe one day . . .'

Davis herself is a living part of that novel's Yankee landscape. Her home is there now: a frame house at Westport, Connecticut, with a view of the Saugatuck River. There she holes up between projects, until restlessness takes her or the tax man calls – 'I'll never be poor, but who can stay rich today without working?'

The landscape, the Episcopalian upbringing, even having Una Merkel to teach her in Sunday School help explain why Plymouth Rock is the spiritual foundation of her professional doughtiness. To her, the Hollywood folk always look as if they have the San Andreas fault built into them and are expecting another earthquake any time.

She doesn't have time to see many of the movies they make these days. *Star Wars*? . . . 'Good luck to it, but it's not my kind of theatre.' but she cheers up slightly on learning that *Julia* and *The Turning Point*, pictures with women at the centre of the interest and the screen, are coming back into prominence. 'There's a tremendous need for that kind of film. They were never exactly plentiful. But in my days at Warners, they did exist to be fought for. Not any more.'

She has a television film she's looking forward to because, well . . . because that's where the 'woman's picture' has gone to. Called *Strangers*, it's the story of a mother whose daughter returns after twenty years' estrangement. She has high hopes that Jane Fonda or Cloris Leachman will play the daughter. 'They're the best of our young players.' And then before she heads for the

Recuperation: *Savoy Hotel, London, 1985*

NEXT TO HOLDING AN INVESTITURE AND bestowing honours on the recipients, no ceremony so becomes Bette Davis as presiding over afternoon tea. But as I entered her hotel suite, I wondered what I should find. News of her mastectomy had been grim ... reports of her recovery contradictory. Had age and illness between them succeeded where Warner Bros had failed in quelling the mutinous spirit of the seventy-six-year-old *grande dame* of Hollywood? I really need not have worried.

Seated on a sofa, back to the river, blonde hair stiffly waved, in a navy dress and white jacket with matching navy spots (by her 'new' California designer David Hayes), she certainly looked smaller and much gaunter. But the words are spat out with the same force. 'Frankly, I *never* thought I'd ever get back to work. But fortunately, the cancer was caught in time. In all my fifty-four years in films, I'd never had a day's fear – but I had that first day back on the set of *Murder by Mirrors*.' (The television film she made in England last November.) 'I feared I'd forget my lines ... that my strength wouldn't last the day out. But it did. I'd spent the summer on Malibu beach, strengthening my legs. If I could stand on them, I told myself, then I could stand up to *anyone*.'

Of course she had had to drop out of *Hotel*, the TV mini-series in which she played a dowager hotelier, and Anne Baxter was brought in to fill the gap. No, the irony of being replaced by Miss Baxter (who played the scheming usurper in *All About Eve*) had not been lost on her. Wasn't that just like life aping art? No? Well then ... aping *bad* art? The howl that would once have greeted this has become a throaty chuckle.

Her first reaction to the news of her illness had been 'immense and immediate relief that I'd done everything in life I'd ever wanted to do. I'd die, if I had to, with no regrets. Now

recuperative breezes of Connecticut, she is taking her one-woman film-show to the West Coast – an hour of clips and then an hour of well-salted, provocative dialogue with audiences whose age gap with hers is closed like carbon arcs igniting when the Davis images spring to life on the screen. They chorus her best-known lines even before that younger Bette Davis wearing the glamour of High Hollywood can let them fall from her lips. The favourite? 'Is there any *competition*?' she asks. And then, with only Max Steiner's dripping score missing, she tilts her head towards an invisible Paul Henreid and articulates *Now, Voyager*'s vibrant last line: 'Oh, Jerry, we have the stars, let's not ask for the moon.'

As I take my leave of Bette Davis, a spry, erect, *sharp* lady, I find myself thinking of another of her films. It was called *The Star* and the poster advertising it had been plastered with a line of that hyperactive copy that almost provokes one into chanting it like those dearly loved passages of dialogue. 'The orchids, the furs,' it ran, '. . . the dreams that were the star's were all gone. Now nothing remained . . . but the woman.' They were wrong, of course. The dreams are all there still. And let's not ask for the orchids and furs. We have the woman.

when poor Bogey got news of *his* cancer – when he was barely fifty-five – his reaction was *anger*. He was *furious* at all he'd be missing. I called my autobiography *The Lonely Life*. On reflection, maybe I've had the lucky life . . . maybe. My greatest stroke of luck was having a child when I did, at the late age of thirty-nine, when my career was made. I could never have sacrificed my work any earlier to start a family. But I had Hollywood *and* children, wasn't *that* something? My biggest disappointment? Oh, the fact that not one of my three marriages went right – a fourth was ended when my husband died suddenly. The others ended in divorce. But then as Mother said, "You can't have everything."' She chuckles at the banality of such a self-denying ordinance.

'When my daughter married a Hyman boy – the Hymans bought Warner Bros, you know, and owned it for a short time – I looked over at her and her husband and thought how *odd* that the old studio where I'd had my monumental battles with Jack L. Warner should come into *my* family. Mr Warner was there when the sale was announced. It was a sad day for him. He signalled me to come over and sit with him, and he took my hand in his,

and he said, nearly crying, "Bette, we're the last ones left." God knows I had my rows with that man. But I owe my *career* to Warners.

'Has Hollywood changed today? Not that I can see. It's just a lot of *different* brothers!'

She has never been idle. If not in films, she has done television movies, or 'worked the chat shows', getting herself the exposure 'that today's bits of stars think they don't need between pictures'. The only part she now really wants to play is Helena Rubinstein. Throughout tea, despite her operation, she smoked continuously, but 'only vegetable cigarettes now', she assured me, manufactured to sate a need, not incur a risk. She took them out of a gold case. I caught sight of an inscription inside it and, with a rasp of the old sarcasm in her voice, she obliged by reading it out: 'An actor is something less than a man, an actress more than a woman.' That seemed to say it all. She stood up to say goodbye and suddenly I saw her thin frame, cruelly diminished by illness – she could not have weighed more than seven stone. A little like a thrush . . . But don't be deceived, I told myself, as I took my leave. That thrush has known the wing-span of an eagle.

2 CHARACTER

EARLY MEMORIES: THEY ARE THE ABIDING ONES. Nearly sixty years later, she could still remember being taken to the circus and seeing that the green carpet covering the ring for the Parade of the Animals had a seam down its length – and it was crooked.

Even aged four or five, Ruth Elizabeth Davis possessed an uncontainable passion for order . . . for perfection. Alone among the hundreds of happy children at the ringside, she bawled her head off at this nagging imperfection which she was powerless to adjust. Years afterwards, in the human circus at Warner Bros, it was a different story. Now she had the power that celebrity conferred on her and she used it to straighten many a seam she considered out of true in the material which the performing animals were assigned to work on.

The need to be in charge can be a fatiguing drive, even a self-destructive obsession. But to Bette Davis, it has always been a source of energy. She never ignored any challenge which life presented, even if the odds were against her or the outcome seldom in doubt. She boldly sought out the most testing opportunities to profit from the system of which she was a part; she exerted will and skill, by repetition and variation, to impress an image of herself and her gender on the world that went to the movies in those days. In over fifty years of film acting, Bette Davis played all kinds and conditions of women. Not that she pretended to be a self-conscious representative of her sex: the times and her individualist's temperament wouldn't have encouraged her to take the spokesperson's role, anyway. Not until the 1940s, a decade after she had won her stardom, did the women who had helped make her a star actually acquire for themselves a piece of that 'power for action' which Davis exemplified in so many bold or subtle ways on the screen. And even then, it took a world war to grant to *them* the sense of fulfilment that Davis had achieved alone in the limited but fierce sorties she fought with her employers.

But once she had learnt how to reconcile her craving for stardom with her contempt for many of its humiliating processes, Davis deployed that hard-earned authority to throw into prominence aspects of the individual women she played in ways that appealed powerfully to the generality of women – and to not a few men as well – over a longer span of years and in a more astonishing variety of roles than any single one of her Hollywood peers. Garbo may have been the rarer being, the purer star: but Garbo eventually vanished into the black hole of 'alone-ness' she had created for herself in the MGM heavens. Joan Crawford was a 'battler', like Davis in that respect. But Crawford carried her clenched desperation over into her roles in ways that limited as well as often brazenly illuminated them. For a time, Dietrich incarnated a potently seductive aspect of womanhood: but it was one that held the men in thrall rather than her own sex. Katharine Hepburn has been Davis's closest rival – and there are some who would refuse to award her the second place. Davis herself always acknowledged the challenge Hepburn represented: but neither woman was ever remotely jealous of the other. Their common New England heritage provided them with the shelter that a good sorority house still offered its girls when they went out into the world: a shared centre of excellence that deterred them from entering into contentious rivalry. Their temperaments appear similar: their ways were surprisingly separate. Hepburn and Davis never made a film together, though it wasn't for the want of trying on Davis's part. Had they done so, it might, like so many summit meetings, have ended in disappointment. Hepburn's persona was that of a born aristocrat. Davis's disposition was to look the lady for a day and then, perversely, engrossingly, to get up the next day feeling like a bitch. Hepburn had the finer consistency. But in matters of stardom, consistency is not everything. Davis's compulsion to play sweet and sour, rational and neurotic, noble and downright mean, devoted and destructive, frightened and aggressive, loving and incapable of love, masculine and feminine, in short to keep expanding her claim on the territory occupied by the modern woman, gave her an ever widening constituency of women to represent.

'No one has ever been better than Davis at her best on the screen,' writes the American critic Richard Schickel. This personal best has always been what she battled for. She was willing to suffer deprivation if the outcome were victory. Her fees were never astronomical (indeed by the standards of other stars, she was underpaid) and her life-style was never flamboyant (for a variety of personal reasons, she tended to live beneath her status). She existed for the power and glory of the part: the fact that, in many cases, the power became the glory doesn't invalidate Bette Davis's claim to an artistic boldness above and beyond the duty roster of a star system that set little store by such individual aspirations and often did its worst to thwart or divert them.

Bette Davis was cast this way from the very start. It wasn't just life that she conceived in terms of a perpetual drama: it was the very act of birth, too. It is maybe unremarkable – though apt – that she should have been born in Lowell, Massachusetts, in 1908, during a thunderstorm. But later on, cataloguing in her autobiography the elements attending her birth in terms of theatre, not meteorology, she made it sound as if she had come into the world from the wings, not the womb. 'I happened between a clap of thunder and a streak of lightning. It almost hit the house and destroyed a tree out front.' To anyone else, except a born actress, that tree would have been simply 'outside'. She made it sound as if it had been occupying the best seat in the house. Acting for her always carried this connotation of elemental force. Long before it meant Hollywood to her, acting meant *power*.

At one time she expressed a desire to play Lewis Carroll's Alice: which sounds strange at first, since Alice is generally considered a

22

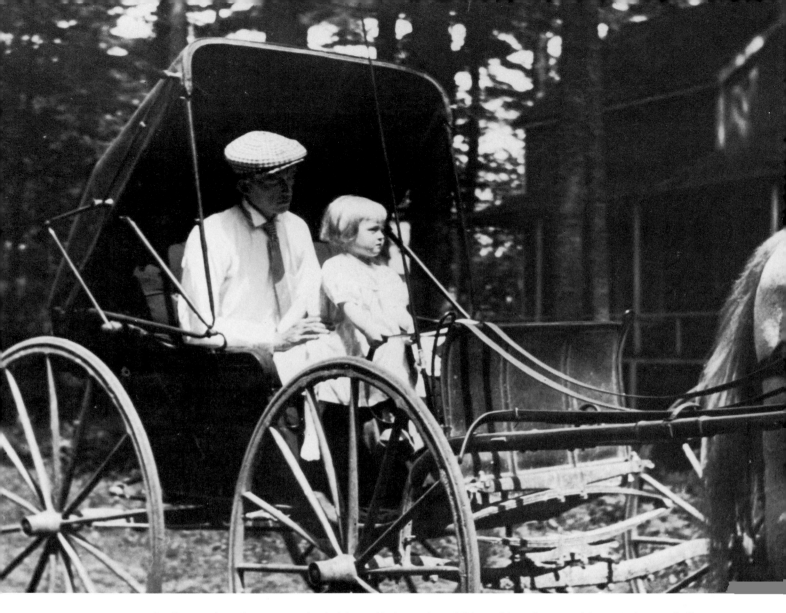

wholly passive character who initiates little and has everything happen to her. But this wasn't how Davis saw the interloper in Wonderland. Alice to her was a girl much like herself: 'a little spitfire . . . rebellious, ferocious, both innocent and cynical, spiritual and intemperate. Alice isn't sweet, she's salty.' In the end, she *did* get to play a heroine much like Carroll's but it was one that went by the name of Jezebel.

It would seem that from an early age she consciously set out to make it difficult for people to love her in the normal way one does a child. Affection wasn't demanded so much as attention. This isn't unusual, however, in children who perceive themselves to be unwanted. Davis's birth was the outcome of accident, not loving premeditation on her parents' part: a slip for which her precise and orderly father was frequently to reproach his wife. Harlow Morell Davis was a practising lawyer with all the neatness of his calling: but what earned him comfortable fees were not the forgivable shortcomings of human nature. Rather, the perfect-

ability of inanimate objects. His speciality was the law of patents. In producing a baby before he desired one, his wife had failed to meet the test of efficiency; and although he fathered a second daughter, Barbara, eighteen months later, this time with planned precision, he could never bring himself to express much spontaneous love for his little family.

Years later, Bette Davis's father unexpectedly appeared in her dressing-room after the first night of one of the early stage roles – and he still found it easier to praise every other member of the cast than her.

Yet this strange man remains more sharply focused than Bette's mother Ruthie, a woman who lived for her daughter every moment of her life – and *with* her daughter for a large stretch of her life until her death at seventy-six. Unable at last to stand her husband's indifference to an all-female household, Mrs Davis braved the shame that came from such marital separations in that puritan community and took herself and her children off to Florida

23

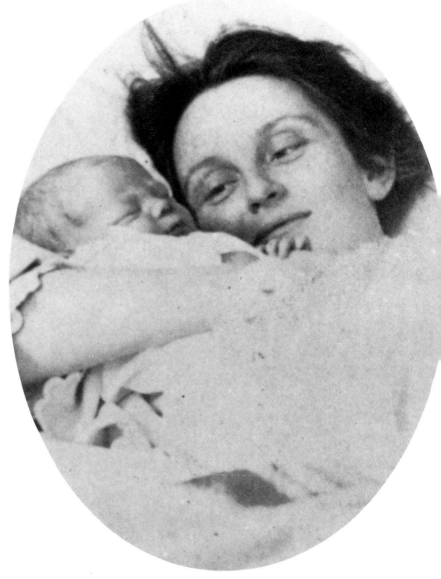

with an Irish nanny for company and home-help. Bette seemed to welcome the break: now they would be free to go on picnics, she said. At this time she was six or seven. And yet it was the characteristics of her absent father that now began asserting themselves in her attitudes to life, the way that some of his physical looks, such as the broad, 'brainy' forehead of the Davises, started to come into prominence in the child's own developing features. That perfectionism she was already showing obviously derived from his side of the family, too. Though she was to dedicate her life to her mother's comfort – just as she dedicated her memoirs 'To Mother, who will always be in the front row' – she actually had far more in common with her father 'off stage'.

When she was Bette's age, her mother Ruthie had been the tomboy of *her* family, the Favors, descendants of English and French Huguenot settlers who had built their church on Quaker bedrock and went on to build a community on hard muscle and stern faith. In her own gentler way, Ruthie was a 'rebel', though she belonged to the Louisa May Alcott school of 'little disturbers'. Her nickname was 'Fred'. She liked taking part in school theatricals. On country outings, she was happier wearing her brother's own tweed pants and shirts. She took easily to painting and home decoration. If it is easy to see a connection here with her daughter's artistry, it is also misleading. Bette's management of her career was a continuous battle to impose order on art and carve perfection out of lumpish material. She denied herself most of the appurtenances of stardom – mansions, limousines, wardrobes, and the like – largely in order to keep *her mother* in the style to which Bette's fans imagined she herself ought to be accustomed. It is all to her credit that she should thus 'nurse' the parent who had done the same for her career: but there was a self-denying passion about it also. While Ruthie enjoyed the vicarious satisfactions of a stardom she hadn't earned, Bette found a more abstemious but rarer satisfaction in *acting*. In short, whether she acknowledged it or not, her character was far closer to her father's than her mother's.

For example, she shared Harlow Davis's determination not to permit other people to deflect his will from its set ways: he is said to have surrendered the chance of a scholarship to study law at Oxford University because, by the strict terms of the benefactor, he would have been required to give up smoking. With him, it wasn't a matter of forfeiting pleasure, but of sticking to principle: and this became his elder daughter's way, too. One can sympathize with this man whose disposition had caused him to retreat farther and farther from a wife whose impulsiveness led to things like picnics and involuntary procreation. He saw self-denial as a source of power. Bette held those puritan certitudes, too.

One scene from childhood is revealing on this score. Bette was behaving so disagreeably to her mother and sister that Mrs Davis suggested to her that they swap clothes and each

Left, after being burned: bandages gained gratifying attention and, right, more than fifty years later, but bandages confirm the player's need to live the part on and off the set of *Phone Call from a Stranger.*

At eighteen, below, taking her Red Cross life-saving test: stamina was needed for stardom, too.

Opposite, in a school play, probably *Miles Standish.*

pretend to be the other. The mother hoped that by seeing her own ill temper reflected in her parent's mime, Bette would reform it accordingly. Instead of which, the thirteen-year-old girl began projecting an icy will-power which soon had her mother giggling nervously. In much the same way her father had asserted his authority round the dinner table before the family had broken up. The disdain that Harlow Davis probably felt for the ordinariness of family life in Lowell reproduced itself in his elder daughter's mischievous play-acting. 'I sensed my power over [my mother],' Bette impenitently recalled. 'My imitation grew greater when she surrendered,' she added with relish. 'There was no holding me.'

The ranks of Hollywood stars have never been swollen by children from happy homes. It is no less true because it is a commonplace that a broken family promotes the sort of personality imbalance that can lay the basis for stardom. When rotated in role after role until a facet of the personality catches the public's eye, focuses its attention, diverts and entertains film-goers and makes them return to see the owner of it in different movies, playing different roles but still gratifyingly identifiable by this recurring characteristic of looks or temperament, then a star is well on the way to being born. Given such circumstances, an unhappy childhood can have its formidable compensations later on. The point is worth stressing. For as one sees the adolescent Bette Davis turning into a conscious artist, one can anticipate how she will extend the power she has tapped in herself, and transform and transcend it inside the studio system that all too often gets the blame for merely truncating it. Sometimes the very resistance that the system shows to a determined individual can be a source of creative energy. 'That wasn't one of my best pictures: I didn't have to fight for it.' Behind this flip sarcasm uttered by Davis in her later days lies the reality of trying to square the economic priorities of the star system that was resistant to change with the reckless ambitions

a medical fact: but it certainly reinforces the myth that has gathered around this emphatic trademark – that it was born out of terror! The Davis orbs have had all kinds of baleful power attributed to them. When a scene needs heightening, they can assume an alarming thyroid effect – one that becomes still more marked if another 'strong' actress happens to be sharing the scene. At other times, when high-definition acting would be a liability, they appear quite normal. This waxing and waning has also been attributed to an attempt to hypnotize other people to do her mental bidding. It was noticed that at the famous legal action which Warner Bros brought against Davis in the English High Court, in 1936, she sat staring fixedly at the judge as if she were willing him to find in her favour. If this is true, then it is one more reason why the statue of justice should wear a blindfold.

Somewhat likelier is the lifelong fascination with making up for the part which that accident to the Santa Claus beard incited.

Unless they are playing a character role or have an obvious need to disguise themselves, most stars remain apprehensive about make-up. *Lighting* – Ah, that is a different matter. Flattering lighting is the star's best friend: make-up tends to be a curse that puts a well-loved image in jeopardy. Not so with Davis. She has relished every opportunity the script gave her – and some she created for herself – to apply the make-up unflinchingly. She is on record as saying she has never considered herself a great beauty: but a readiness to hide behind the greasepaint isn't the whole or indeed the likely truth. Undeniably, the outer realism contributes to the inner logic of her acting. One of the earliest (and most infamous) examples of her predilection for 'wearing' the character both outside and in occurred when she played Mildred, the consumptive tramp-heroine in *Of Human Bondage*. The pale and wasted complexion of someone denied air and light by her job as a waitress had an occupational reality. And as her constitution weakens,

of an artist who thrived on challenge. Charles Laughton put it very well when he passed by the set of a Davis picture one day and, smelling battle in the air, gleefully added his pinch of gunpowder to the explosive situation. 'Never stop daring to hang yourself, Bette,' he advised.

She probably savoured the sweet authority of the star-actress while she was still a child. While playing Santa Claus at a school Christmas party the cotton-wool beard she was wearing caught fire, and for a few delicious minutes she pretended to have been blinded by the flames. Witnessing everyone's terror conveyed a completeness of command that she had never before known; and the fright her mother got at seeing her daughter being returned to her in a cocoon of bandages was sheer undiluted joy.

In other ways, too, it was a formative moment. Mrs Davis bathed her child's burnt face in boric acid. Later on she asserted that this treatment had somehow contributed to Bette's most prominent feature – her unusually protuberant eyes. This is extremely doubtful as

Learning physical control: as The Moth in one of the speciality dances taught her by Roshanara.

Opposite left, the contemporary caption (c. 1926) reads: 'Bette Davis, the daughter of attorney Harlow Davis, of Boston, has been selected by John Murray Anderson as the ideal modern Venus. She is a blonde with delicate features and well-proportioned figure. J. M. Anderson is the leading theatrical producer in the United States, and conducted the search for the modern Venus for many months.' This was probably mother's official portrait of her successful daughter – and it reads like mother's official version of events, too.

Bette at seventeen or eighteen (right): already showing the famous eyes.

her predatory nature grows in desperation. Davis insisted on doing her own make-up for her death scene, suspecting it was here, if anywhere, that the studio executives would try to soften her self-lacerating impression of a part that had initially been considered too 'unsympathetic' for any unblemished star to consider playing. Jack L. Warner's alarm when he viewed Mildred in the last stages of disintegration gave her the same malicious satisfaction as her schoolmates had provided when her beard went up in smoke at that Christmas party. The ointments, emulsions and bandages her mother applied over the weeks to young Bette's burnt face established the pleasure of making up for the part later on. Once those bandages came off, she noted, interest in her condition faded; conversely, once the make-up went on, she re-focused attention. A burnt child usually dreads fire: this one celebrated it.

The months after Mrs Davis quit the family home, accompanied by her children, had been restless ones. They moved from one lodging-house to the next, since her strict Episcopalian relatives were not disposed to offer accommodation to a woman who had voluntarily left her husband. By the time they had softened their attitude and Ruthie's divorce had gone through, she and her family had been to some eighty addresses – at least according to the private memoir she later wrote – and had accepted rootlessness as a way of life. This may help account for the mental restlessness that kept Davis perpetually on the go in later life, not only from house to house but from part to part. Her Yankee ancestry was to draw her back again and again to the safe harbour scenery of the East Coast, but she never dropped anchor there for any length of time. Work took her back West. The New England-type homes she re-created there, under California's sun, were an idealized part of the past that stood for those settled decencies of well-rooted community life so alien to the Hollywood ethos where everything is in transition. 'But in itself, a home gave me no peace of mind. That came

through work: and then, only rarely.'

Her mother had enrolled her at the age of ten in a school in the Berkshires, a rural stretch of New England, which was run on energetic outdoor lines that sometimes obliged the pupils to wear mittens indoors, too, against the wintry nip of its classrooms. It was just as well that she was hardened by the natural elements: for the production files of her Warner films testify to the unrelenting pressure of work at that studio. The 'Dream Factory' was indeed a *factory*. In spite of her seasoned constitution, Davis suffered from an usual variety of ailments over the years there, all of them precisely set down for insurance or contractual reasons in the studio memoranda. It may well be that only in this way could her constitution 'appeal' against the injustice of what she considered incompetent direction, poor scripts or simply the oppressiveness of the high-powered system. There were few other ways that stars could protest in those days. The 'slave contract' then in operation meant that the studio owned them,

body and soul, over a precisely specified duration of months and years, and absences from work due to a refusal to comply with the conditions of employment simply led to the time spent on suspension being added on to the terminal date of the contract. It was essentially a form of peonage and was not repealed until the mid-1940s, and then by actually invoking the peonage system that had once been illegally applied to Mexican labourers in California. But one means of protest possessed by a star to show that he or, more likely, she was unhappy, was allowing the body to give way to the soul's sickness. Davis's 'protests' over a decade or more were no doubt sincere and well based in medical fact – certainly they were painful enough – but if her metabolism hadn't been made so resilient by her Yankee upbringing, it's hard to believe she could have borne all the ailments she suffered and which, in turn, were visited upon her employers in more calculable forms.

Bette's natural bent for 'dramatics' was stimulated by several events in her early years as a teenager. Ruthie's ambitions for her child often led her to fortune tellers. It is not surprising that they told this anxious mother with the little girl in tow that the child would make a mark in the world – or that the mother should interpret it as meaning the world of the theatre. To this end, Ruthie began getting professional training for Bette even before she went to college. Around the age of fifteen, she began attending a dance academy, Mariarden, at Peterboro, New Hampshire, and there she met one of her most influential teachers, an Englishwoman called Jane Craddock who went by the professional name of 'Roshanara' in order to give a communicable coloration of Eastern dance and rhythm to her instruction, which was otherwise delivered in crisp British tones. Indeed her teacher's accent was what first struck Bette about her: it was made for issuing orders. Roshanara's talents ran to design as well as dance instruction. She was a friend of Natasha Rambova, who had been

Rudolph Valentino's second wife and a woman of great artistry whose stage name likewise concealed a less exotic identity as plain Winifred Shaunessy. By coincidence, Roshanara had designed the sets of *The Green Goddess*, which had starred George Arliss, another figure of great influence in Davis's career. The omens were being assembled around her.

Roshanara based her teaching on the rhythms of Indian dancing; but the body movement was intended to express more than grace. Pupils were expected to attune themselves to the whole rhythm of their body so that they could think themselves into the emotion or the character they were expressing. Bette was so successful in the end-of-term performances that a stage career was confidently predicted for her. For a child (and a mother) already in love with the notion of a 'destined' life, it was all additional confirmation. Bette's grandmother had urged her to 'believe in something. Work for it. It will be yours.' The key word here was 'work'. In Hollywood, where fantasies encouraged much the same sort of positive thinking, the word that all too often applied was 'wish'. It may have been the same relative who suggested to the child that she spell her name 'Bette', derived from Balzac's novel *Cousine Bette*, though still pronounced 'Betty'. 'It will set you apart,' she was told. Her strength of will was already doing that.

She was more conscious of her looks than ever; for her mother had begun supplementing the frugal allowance she got from her family by taking on assignments as a part-time photographer – wedding and school groups, etc – which allowed her to do a lot of the retouching work at home. Here, too, the daughter saw, 'perfection' was an end. Bette sometimes 'stood in' for the subject while her mother was arranging the portrait lighting. She was well aware that she wasn't a conventional beauty: head too round, eyes too large, neck too long, looking indeed like Tenniel's sketches of Alice in Wonderland.

In 1924, when she was sixteen, she began attending co-ed classes at Cushing Academy, in Ashburnham, Mass., where the presence of boys dispelled her sexual innocence without tempting her to yield to the experience. She was drawn to one young man who was personable in the passive sort of way that posed no threat. Their affections centred round the glee club and college theatricals. She threw herself into acting any role she was offered; and Harmon Oscar Nelson, a gawky, good-natured youth, sang, composed and played the cornet and piano. He was to become Bette Davis's first husband and, if her account is to be believed, left his middle name to movie history more memorably than his marriage since his wife dubbed the first Academy Award statuette she won an "Oscar" – perhaps because the then nameless figurine's facelessness represented what her marriage had come to resemble. Another version has it that the "Oscar" was named by an Academy official after her uncle. Davis has said, characteristically, that those who wish to believe that, can do.

At this time, however, she was working her way through college in the traditional manner by waiting on tables. Initially, she had felt the work to be beneath her dignity. 'At that point in my life, I was extremely sure of one's station ... A waitress was on one level, a doctor on another, and so on.' By the time she made *Of Human Bondage*, she had learnt that a waitress's neurotic attachment to a doctor could eliminate the inequalities of class and even feed off them. Early lessons were once again put to good use.

On her graduation, the family moved to a tiny apartment in New York: getting Bette's stage career launched was now the first priority. But immediately it met with a set-back. The drama school run by the distinguished actress Eva Le Gallienne turned her down. The circumstances are unclear; and if Miss Le Gallienne later remembered the nervous girl at all, she was unwilling to concede that she had been wrong in her advice to get herself a shop-girl's job. Perhaps Bette (or her mother) was simply

o much' and came on 'too strong'. Perhaps
e test piece in which she had to read the part
an elderly Dutch peasantwoman shook the
ginner's confidence, as it may have been
ant to do in order to 'discourage the others'
o were knocking at the door. Fortunately
e John Murray Anderson school of drama
ved the day – and the peace of mind of a child
o was driving herself into a near-breakdown
er this precipitate rejection. Anderson's
ool specialized in developing its pupils'
ight into themselves as much as into the
es they played. Insight, but *not* empathy: it
mportant to understand this, for Davis was
ver an exponent of the technique that
uired one to *become* the part. She was
ght to work from the inside out and to
velop the self-awareness necessary to project
character and 'irradiate' it. The Method,
course, in the early and uncorrupted form
it codified by Stanislavsky, was intended to
se the performer's sense of being by means
sets of exercises – it was not intended that
player should *lose* his being by sinking it
isibly into the role. Davis and her fellow
pils were helped to articulate their own styles
l keep them visible. This may well have nar-
ved the range of parts available to them, but
compensation was a great gain in expres-
eness. Joan Blondell, Lucille Ball, Cesar
mero, Anita Page and Paul Muni were
ong the students; and Muni proved an early
l brilliant forerunner of the American vari-
on of The Method by changing his looks and
ure over a wide range of characters and thus
ming omnipotent, yet oddly remote, in a
llywood which thrived on stars who could
predicted to look like themselves in role
er role.

his set Davis a problem, too, when she got
Hollywood and became a star. How could
take to playing a radically different role
hout forfeiting her mass appeal? Her
nnerisms' sometimes drew criticism: yet
y were part of the solution she developed.
tardom was a way of standardizing the

familiar, then acting was a way of nuancing it.

One of her teachers at this time was Martha Graham, who promulgated the creed, 'To dance is to act.' Once more, emphasis was placed on the *whole* body of the player, even if the visible emotion was centred only on the part of it that was to interest the camera. Even in her early supporting roles, Davis was not much impressed by stars whose emotions ended at their neck-line. Whenever she climbed or descended a staircase in any of her films, she proudly noted that it was Martha Graham 'step by step'.

She graduated from the Anderson school in a play called *The Famous Mrs Fair*, as a sweet young thing who goes to pieces in the aftermath of the First World War and turns into an embittered old woman: an eerie preview of the 'Mrs Skeffington' role she was to play in the films. Separated at last from her mother's vigilance, she took small roles in a series of plays put on by stock-companies in the North-Eastern states, one of them run by George Cukor, the future film director. Surprisingly, he and Davis did not get on well together. He later said that what made him uncomfortable was the excess of neurotic energy he felt she travelled on: she acted 'with her nerves'. She brought herself up to pitch by seemingly *willing* the audience that saw her playing a moll in the musical drama *Broadway* to believe that she actually had shot her lover's killer in the back. By curious accident, Marlene Dietrich was producing a similarly electric effect playing the very same role in the production of *Broadway* in Vienna not many months earlier in 1927. Dietrich, we may be sure, took killing for love far more coolly.

Davis's engagement lasted not much more than a week and she travelled round other companies, playing a succession of negligible parts, though learning to curb something of her nervous display of energy after a rebuke from Laura Hope Crews, one of those theatrical battle-axes who took the matriarchal roles in Hollywood in the 1930s. Then she returned to

the Cukor company and was engaged as a young wife in *Excess Baggage*. It had Miriam Hopkins in the lead. Thus was established, early and lastingly, a rivalry between two remarkable actresses based on the cold-blooded appreciation that each had of the other's ability to dominate a scene. In the films they were to make together, their contest of wills was supplemented by every technical wile they possessed to retain the focus of the audience's interest or sympathy. Hopkins's talent was formidable, though Davis scored many a diplomatic victory by openly acknowledging it, indeed lauding it, whenever interviewers came round to it. But her nature wasn't a 'giving' one, and somehow audiences sensed this and refused her the ultimate accolade of stardom. Bette, in Laughton's words, always dared to hang herself: Hopkins prepared the noose for others.

After she had appeared in four more plays, Cukor abruptly terminated Davis's engagement. The reason had more to do with stock-company politics than professional short-comings. The truth was, she wasn't prepared to 'socialize'. Her dedication left no place for the intimacies to which an *ingénue* was expected to respond, if not actually invite. As she bluntly expressed it later, she was supposed to be 'public domain'. Louis Calhern, another member of the company, accused her of being 'so grimly dedicated to work that it became boring . . . it didn't make for comfort in an incestuous company like that. She was a terrific team *player*, but she wasn't a team *person*.' But she quickly rebounded from this upset when James Light, a theatre director and guest lecturer at the Anderson drama school, put her into his Greenwich Village production of *The Earth Between*, as a Southern girl whose transcendent innocence takes the taint out of her father's too closely affectionate attachment to her. The critics were called from their Broadway beat to witness the production on the strength of Light's reputation, and they caught her performance and praised it. It is hard, however, to spy the future Bette Davis in Brooks Atkinson's description of 'an entrancing creature' with a 'soft unassertive style'.

The excellent notices she received caught the eye of Blanche Yurka. Miss Yurka was an acknowledged figure of power on the New York stage, with a high reputation for her interpretations of Ibsen heroines which she enhanced by her own liberated style of life. As a child, Davis had seen and been excited by her production of *The Wild Duck*. Now she found herself being asked to play Hedwig in it.

As she played the unwanted child rejected by her father, it seemed to her that she was moving into areas of her own life: it can only have added to the pathos that won critical praise. The *Washington Post*'s critic who wrote of her 'native sweetness' and 'spiritual wholesome-

ness' reminds us of one useful corrective to the later film image of Bette Davis. Namely, this was how Hollywood expected her to be when, not many months ahead, she was to present herself to the movie company that had brought her out to the Coast on the advice of a talent scout in far-away New York. In other words, they were not prepared for what they found; and she, fresh from the experience of playing 'sweet', 'wholesome' and 'spiritual' roles, was dismayed to find that they wished her to transplant qualities that weren't at all native to her into the minor film roles that didn't call for much else. Hence their puzzled irritation and her deeper dismay and profound despondency. Though by all accounts, she made a 'profoundly sympathetic and appealing' Hedwig, her ambitions must have been keyed to the far more dramatic display she saw Blanche Yurka giving in the leading role in *The Wild Duck*. A lot of the mannerisms of this authoritative actress were ones that became characteristic of Davis – especially her emphatic gestures and the way she bit off her words as if they were attached to her by an umbilical cord.

It is strange how three of the greatest film actresses, all contemporaries in Hollywood, but not known to have sought each other's company there or even to have met except by chance, had their styles influenced during their impressionable years by 'strong' women who were their intimate friends or professional acquaintances. When Greta Garbo was only months away from having to make her debut in the talkies, in 1930, she sought the company of a Swedish actress, Naima Wifstrand, who knew how to speak English, and, consciously or not, absorbed the deeper tones of this Lapland woman into her own fateful manner of speaking. Dietrich, too, appearing in a Berlin musical in 1926, is reputed to have carried away an echo of the low, almost gruff singing voice of Claire Waldoff, the *chanteuse* who reflected the sexual ambiguities of Berlin cabaret life. Davis's tour with Blanche Yurka's company lasted a couple of months, alternating her role

in *The Wild Duck* with one of the young sisters in Ibsen's *The Lady from the Sea*, and her tutelage by an actress whose own large eyes and impatient gestures enhanced their kindred relationship in the play, surely helped confirm her style and later acting preferences. And she was given a taste for something that could be satisfied more immediately. Blanche Yurka allowed this relative beginner to take a solo curtain, an untypically generous gesture and one that testifies to the strength of the impression that Davis must have made on her patron and the audience. Davis heard the applause and remembered that moment as if it were an epiphany: 'I was alone – on stage and everywhere ... and that is the way it was always meant to be.'

Two more plays followed with other com-

panies, *Broken Dishes* (1929) and *Solid South* (1930), both domestic comedies, both star vehicles for, respectively, Donald Meek and Richard Bennett (father of Constance, Joan and Barbara Bennett), and both offering her well-taken opportunities to play sweet, sometimes high-tempered girls. She received notices that caught the attention of the casting agents who were then scouring Broadway on Hollywood's behalf recruiting talent for 'the talkers', as the new-ish sensation of sound pictures was still being called.

The studios were desperate to sign up anyone who had acting experience based on the delivery of lines. Such had been the initial panic when the talkies were seen to have come to stay and the stars of the silents had almost been thought of as natural mutes – and expensive leading ladies and gentlemen had been shipped West from Broadway to replace them. Of course, the public had preferred the screen favourites it already knew, in spite of (and indeed because of) their untrained voices; but fresh faces as much as new voices were now in demand for the greater social realism – especially *American* realism – that the talkies were imposing on stories and stars.

Davis had already one screen test behind her: it had been made on a freezing sound stage in the Astoria Studios on Long Island. Sam Goldwyn had been seeking an actress to play in *Raffles* opposite Ronald Colman, whose usual leading lady, Vilma Banky, could no longer be plausibly teamed with him due to her Hungarian-accented English. Now as Raffles was an English gentleman-crook and the film's setting was English 'high society', Goldwyn's talent scout probably recommended Davis on account of her clipped diction with its connotation of lady-like Englishness – or so it might sound to American ears, anyhow. But she was badly recorded during the test, poorly lit and thoroughly ill at ease: it made her think of the artificial poses she had had to hold as a 'stand-in' at sessions in her mother's photography business. The shock she got when she saw the test shook her confidence even more because, probably for the first time, she saw her features *in motion* and discovered she had a lop-sided way of speaking – as well as a slightly crooked front tooth. Her disenchantment was echoed more explosively by Goldwyn. 'What are you trying to do to me?' he shouted when the test was run: and that ended that.

Davis was not too upset. She was stage- and not star-struck. Talkies were still thought beneath the dignity of true stage artists, though this was a view that the increasing sophistication of the medium changed within months.

The almost weekly arrival of new talking pictures on Broadway proved the revolution wasn't going to go away – and had better be joined while there was still room in the ranks. Some of Davis's fellow players and near contemporaries had already done so, among them Paul Muni, Joan Blondell, James Cagney and even Miriam Hopkins. The lowest scale of Hollywood pay was two to three times what Broadway could afford. Moreover, mother and daughter had never forgotten the fortune teller who had prophesied that Bette would be known all over the world: surely that meant the talkies?

So when a second screen test followed her success in *Solid South*, she approached it with rather more enthusiasm (as well as a freshly straightened front tooth). She played a brief scene from one of the winter season's successful comedies, Preston Sturges's *Strictly Dishonourable*; and on the basis of this, David Werner, a talent scout for Universal Pictures, took it on himself to offer her a movie contract. The repetition of a stage role probably eased her into the photographic test much more comfortingly than the poses which Goldwyn's representative had required her to strike. And so, on 8 December 1930, Bette and her mother, with a pet terrier on a leash and all of fifty-seven dollars in their purses, entrained on the five-day journey to Hollywood. Their arrival wasn't auspicious. The low-ranking Universal employee deputed to meet them quite failed to recognize the pair and later compounded what their nervous and insecure mood had seen as a snub by explaining that he had expected to see an actress. 'Hadn't I a dog with me?' the 'actress' asked tartly. It is the first recorded sarcasm that Bette Davis let fall on California soil: later, of course, she was to scatter them in profusion.

3 BATTLE

IN THE MATTER OF HER HOLLYWOOD EMPLOYERS, Davis had little choice. But she knew that a contract with Universal that started at 350 dollars a week testified to hope rather than status. The studio was then enjoying the profit and prestige of its pacifist war epic *All Quiet on the Western Front*, which had been released a few months before Davis's arrival. A year later, in 1931, it would strike the hugely lucrative mine of Gothic fantasy with *Dracula* and *Frankenstein*, though the horror genre actually represented a small part of its output. It had 'women's directors' like John Stahl on its payroll: Davis would soon be working with him. What it didn't have, however, was any skill or even propensity for creating women stars. Carl Laemmle, its founder, and his son, known as 'Junior', who managed the studio in Laemmle Senior's frequent absences, shared no vision of desirable womanhood – 'desirable' meaning all gradations from the 'divine' downwards. Other Hollywood moguls, like Mayer and Thalberg (at MGM), Jack L. Warner (at Warner Bros) and Harry Cohn (at Columbia), created female images on the screen out of their own immigrant nostalgia for Europe or the vernacular of their adoptive America.

All that Universal did for Davis at first was to heap indignity upon indifference. She was put through yet another screen test – to determine her 'type'.

Now a screen test was the only means – and a rough one it was, too – of estimating a player's potential; and it was the common experience of all but the best established newcomers to feel that such tests invalidated their personality rather than established it. Actresses with stage experience felt particularly humiliated when they were vetted for appearance, not ability. The assistant directors or photographers usually assigned to make the tests itemized the imperfections of bodies that hadn't yet acquired a personality that had been groomed to improve them. For her test, Davis had to stand up to – or, rather, lie down before – a succession of second-string male players who pretended to seduce her. Even though she was the one being put to the test, the camera appeared to be favouring *them*! By thus raping her dignity almost before she was through the studio gates, this initiation ceremony confirmed her life-long dislike of entrusting herself to people for whom she had no respect. The sarcasm and mistrust she later vented on the male sex on and off screen were probably fed by a festering memory of these early indignities. Her nervousness made her edgy, snappish and impatient with people who thought of life in terms of moving pictures: she was suffering early symptoms of what a later age would call 'culture shock'.

Bette and her mother, who were soon joined by Bette's sister Barbara, had moved into a Grimms-style cottage, typical of the architectural fantasies that aped their owners' source of livelihood; and they already regretted exchanging the exuberance and camaraderie of New York life for this hot and culturally arid film capital. This, too, was the customary reaction of transplanted foreign talents. Garbo had felt the desiccation of the place in the climate as well as its culture; Dietrich had been depressed by its provincialism of spirit as well as location. And *they* were able to seek the consolation of fellow expatriates in the foreign colonies in and around the studios. Bette 'retired into herself', according to her mother, her spirits drooping, any thirst for fame unslaked. Joan Crawford, who had arrived in Hollywood five years earlier with fewer talents, had been better prepared for what awaited her. She came to MGM as much a fan as a budding star: she stepped into the dream, and it enclosed her for life.

Back East, Davis hadn't been a frequent movie-goer: the reigning stars simply didn't interest her. Now that she was in a place where rank and privileges were fixed by the success of one's last picture, and not by well-established stage pre-eminence, she felt excluded . . . powerless. The best cure was work. But what was she to be put to work on?

Her first Hollywood home, built in Grimms' fairytale style and described in the studio caption as 'one of the most unique (sic) and interesting' in the film colony. One of the most cramped, too.

Not yet a film star, right, but already a fashion plate: 'Pretty Bette Davis,' ran the caption, 'wears a one-piece sport dress and a short-sleeved red velveteen jacket, belted.'

Opposite, Bette at home: one of the first of many moments spent on a staircase; others were more dramatic, the stairs grander.

38

'What kind of star have we hired?' While the front office pondered, Universal's portrait photographer tried out the poses.

And opposite, another studio portrait: the profile was also unconventional.

What continued to perplex her Universal employers was the nature of her appeal. What 'type' was she? Again, this indecision wasn't uncommon in Hollywood then – or even later. Indeed some studios only discovered that they had such and such a player of promise on their roster – even in their studio, awaiting assignment – when they saw the studio portraits of him or her published in periodicals like *Vanity Fair* which had had them taken when the person of promise first arrived in New York. MGM had left Garbo to languish for weeks in their Culver City studio until they spotted what could be done with her from a photo taken by a New York photographer a month or so earlier. In any case, it wasn't the people in the front office who 'made' a star: it was the mass public. Hence the history of stardom is littered with examples of movie companies only realizing they had a star among them when the box-office Annunciation identified her or cinema

managers, reacting to their patrons' preference, insisted on revising the poster billing and put the chosen one's name above the title.

It is arguable that Bette Davis went to Hollywood a fatal year or two too soon. Her New York stage success had given her a reputation as an actress of promise. But had she stayed on and played another couple of Broadway seasons, she would almost certainly have established herself, found her 'form' and set her 'style' – and in all likelihood would have been able to dictate her terms to the movie studios the way Katharine Hepburn was to do in 1932, when David Selznick was prepared to pay her 1,500 dollars a week to star in her first film: the fee reflected her *theatrical* stardom. Davis came to Hollywood on *their* terms, not hers: and years went by before Hollywood reluctantly granted her the power to dictate her demands and be rewarded proportionately.

There had been little financial risk in laying out money on a 'promising' Easterner like Davis. The money actually paid her was small change: more a wager on her form than wages for her efforts. It could be easily cut off if the option on her services were not picked up. It was cruelly one-sided.

Davis didn't fit into the conventional categories of the beautiful or the sexy. Even her hair was darker than the then fashionable tones of the 'gold-digger'. So instead of playing the eponymous *Bad Sister* of her first film and perhaps setting the style to which she would later accustom one, this 'little brown wren', as she struck Universal executives, was cast as the *good* sister who confides her own love for her spoiled sister's young man to the pages of her diary – until the foolish sibling gets her comeuppance and leaves the way free for true love and virtue. *Bad Sister* had odd similarities with a film that Davis was to make eleven years later, *In This Our Life*, directed by John Huston, with Olivia de Havilland cast as her sister: but by then she had established an indisputable claim to 'badness'. It was de Havilland who had to make do with virtue.

The story goes – and, thanks to Davis's gleeful repetition of it in a myriad interviews, has 'gone' for decades – that Carl Laemmle Jr's comment on her first film performance was the withering observation that she had about as much sex appeal as Slim Summerville, an ex-Keystone comic specializing in 'cornball' roles: he was also in the cast of *Bad Sister*. But Karl Freund, who had photographed it, was kinder: at least she had lovely eyes, he said, and thus supposedly saved her from the sack.

What was happening here is very likely what had already happened in the Cukor stock company: Davis's air of withdrawal, her seriousness in the midst of casual make-believe, was interpreted as stand-offishness. She had been made to wear a low-cut cotton dress in the film, to make her look more 'interesting' and she felt she had been valued for what was euphemistically called her 'chest', rather than her art. She had felt 'common'. Worse, perhaps, she had felt so excessively virtuous in the role that 'it turned my stomach'. And worst of all, where was the reward? 'All that nobility, and what did it get me? The second lead.'

In such quick succession that she had no time to protest – not that anyone would have listened – she was cast in five more films, usually as somebody's daughter, sister or girl-friend. In two of them, she was a 'loan-out' to other studios: a sure sign of an employer making a contract player 'pay her way' by being hired out at a slight profit, rather than take the trouble and the risk of trying to make her into a star in its own pictures. She had begun salting the Press interviews she was lined up to give with some cutting references to this lack of interest in her, implying that it had been a mistake to come three thousand miles west of Broadway – and set her career back by three years: none of which helped endear her to Universal. And then, unexpectedly, Broadway came to her. . . .

It came in the unexpectedly gentlemanly shape of George Arliss, then one of the most respected persons in Hollywood. Two years

earlier, in 1929, Arliss had helped the talkies attain the status of entertainment for the discriminating. It is not generally appreciated that many people took against the early talkies when they began arriving in sufficient numbers to start driving the silent films off the screen and into the most swift and total eclipse that any art form has ever suffered. The usurper entertainment was deemed rackety and vulgar: it talked the language of the streets, the ghetto and the gutter. But with his precise diction and vocally 'superior' English accent, Arliss helped legitimize the new-fangled medium the way that Adolph Zukor's importing of 'famous players' from the stage had attempted to do, with some success, in the second decade of the century. Arliss's first talkie, *Disraeli*, made for Warners in 1929, satisfied the innovators' hunger for 'class', that intangible quality Hollywood can recognize when it comes calling, but never seems able to breed at home. Arliss thus inherited the prestige belonging to Emil Jannings, the German star of some of the last Hollywood 'silents', who had gone home to 'meet the enemy' in his own tongue first. By 1931, Arliss's tongue was still a golden one: his prestige gave him many more rights than the average star when Warner Bros proposed a talkie remake of one of his most popular silent successes, *The Man Who Played God*. This fastidious man was granted power to approve the director, to select the cast and to 'oversee' the production. Among his early priorities was finding an actress young enough to play his platonic sweetheart in the film, yet experienced enough to match his own exacting standards of acting and enunciation. He found Bette Davis. How he did so matters little: some say she came recommended by an actor friend of Arliss's who had been in one of her 'loan-out' films; Darryl F. Zanuck, then head of production at Warners, always claimed later that he suggested her. The point is, 'Mr George Arliss' (as he was billed) *approved* her. He was then sixty-two: she was twenty-three.

Though he could be a martinet to work with, Arliss's manners were still those of a courtly late Victorian. The courtesy he showed to Davis, coupled with a fatherly concern for a girl who hadn't known a father of her own since she was eight, made her feel wanted and appreciated for the first time since she had come to Hollywood. Universal, she said later, had tested her for her legs: Arliss wanted to examine her soul. What is somewhat likelier, if less poetic, is that Arliss's British reserve deterred him from giving her a screen test for either body *or* soul. He intended rehearsing the film for a week in advance of shooting: if Davis did not measure up, there was time to replace her. Moreover, she was not exactly an unknown quantity to him. He had been a guest lecturer (in diction, naturally) at the Anderson school of drama: he had also seen her on the stage and in at least one of her movies. If she had seen any of *his* films, Davis has left no comment on it: but then a stage reputation always meant more to her than fame gained on the screen, and Arliss was still a renowned stage player. His considerateness next took a very practical turn. He insisted that she have her hair cut shorter and dyed to a lighter tone. This made for a screen appearance much closer to life: hitherto, the lighting had made her hair look even darker than it was.

Arliss's own emphasis on good diction can only have confirmed her already emphatic pronunciation. The story (which may be apocryphal) has it that she couldn't believe it was the great George Arliss calling when he telephoned to offer her the role, and tried to turn the joke on the caller by imitating his very British accent. But he gave her another lesson that was even worthier of imitation: he showed her how to use power. For the first time she stood by the side of a player who was exercising the imperatives of a producer – much more intelligently, too, than any producer she had yet known! It was a tempting example to set a girl who needed only confidence and opportunity to let her own strong will show its teeth. The concern she later showed with every detail

of her movies – from the testing of a co-star (Paul Henreid in *Now, Voyager*) to approving a co-star's hair-cut (Glenn Ford in *A Stolen Life*) – reflected those early days as the autocrat's apprentice.

Viewed today, *The Man Who Played God* (1932) resembles an inspirational version of Hitchcock's *Rear Window*: it might be re-titled *Front Window*. For the famous concert artist Monty Royale (Arliss) who is rendered deaf by an anarchist's bungled attempt to assassinate a music-loving monarch by a bomb, compensates for his handicap by lip-reading the conversations of lonely people in the park below his penthouse with the aid of binoculars, and then using his wealth to change (and even save) their lives. Coming at the peak of the American Depression, when millions could have done with a little of this remote but pragmatic philanthropy, *The Man Who Played God* was conceived as a 'consolation' film. Hollywood was evincing some justifiable anxiety over its own protected status as a refuge from reality and cast itself in the role of a mediator between the 'haves' and the 'have nots'. Screwball comedies reconciling the poor to their misfortunes by showing that the rich had their troubles, too, were less sentimentalized examples of the same attempt to divert the potential anger of the workless masses into laughter or tears. The film, in addition, was an excellent vehicle for Arliss. By surrounding himself from the start with adoring women friends, while not failing to allude to his own years, he disarms the audience's first objection – and his charm quickly converts scepticism into warmer feeling. The wistful affection of this old smoothie may be self-centred, but it narrows the age gap between himself and his young fiancée, played by Davis. Even so, it leaves Davis to negotiate the pitfalls of the ambiguous middle-ground occupied by a girl who looks young enough to be Arliss's daughter but has an emotional commitment to become his wife. Interestingly, perhaps predictably, she is rather better at expressing a daughterly sense of solicitude for

47

Arliss than she is at making reluctant protestations to the suitor of her own age who keeps the park bench warm for her. (Arliss, of course, lip-reads their affair from his balcony.) In her scenes with Arliss, he is like a tuning fork: she vibrates touchingly, but it is he who strikes the note. In the arms of her young lover, finding it uncongenial to take her 'pitch' from him, she becomes shrill and precipitate. But she shows she has already mastered what became one of her best-known 'tricks' – draining her face of vivacity simply by not opening her eyes to their full extent.

The film ends with age sacrificing itself to youth – 'I admire you more than I love you,' says the ever gentlemanly Arliss, indicating that the boy in the park will get the proportions right. But the two of them are so well matched that one wonders whether this solution was met with popular consent. Mary Pickford, faced with a not dissimilar dilemma in *Daddy Long Legs*, decided to end the film with her veritable child throwing herself bodily into the lap of her elderly courtier-guardian's lap. Arliss, a wise old bird, clearly decided that self-sacrifice was the better part of stardom.

One really cannot over-emphasize what Davis learned from this artful as well as artistic man. Arliss has been called a 'ham'. He was nothing of the sort, at this time anyhow. He noted that Davis already knew how to concentrate on a role: he added something even more useful in a film career, and especially in the career of someone set on being an *actress*, as distinct from stars who simply settled for 'being themselves'. Arliss taught her how to maintain the continuity of a character, working it out in her mind in advance of shooting, then protecting the integrity of emotion and looks against the jigsaw method of filming and editing. What she was getting was an education not just in proficiency: but in power, too.

With Arliss's encouragement, Warner Bros signed Davis to a long-term contract, probably to the relief of Universal, which made a small profit on the transfer. Warners was a high-pressure place. The studio paid its artists less than Paramount or MGM; it worked them harder; it promoted them to star status with reluctance, fearing to give 'the workers' power'; its production line under Darryl F. Zanuck turned out between thirty-five and forty films yearly. These called for high-definition, hard-edged acting. Warner characters generally knew where they fitted into American society: that place was in the class that worked or, owing to the Depression, wanted to work but couldn't. The moral, social and economic tenets of Middle America, shaken by people's loss of confidence in the primary values of life under the Depression, and especially the lack of jobs, were condensed and personalized into melodramas of an individual's fate. Warners got the reputation of a strong social conscience: in reality, its 'conscience' was simply the moral collateral of the traditional 'happy ending', with the unhappiness providing the drama being refracted through the social unrest of the times. Warners therefore wanted stars who looked like 'people' and films that looked like 'life', though in both cases 'life' and 'people' had to conform to the demands of popular entertainment. The art of reconciling them was the concern of writers, producers directors – and players. One never thinks of Warner female players as 'goddesses', the way one does of the ladies at MGM or Paramount.

Bette Davis certainly never, at any time, thought of herself that way. Her goal was reality, not divinity. And by making the move to Warner Bros, she had begun to swim with the realist current. All too soon, realizing it was a 'reality' defined by the male world of her employers, she would begin to swim against it. For the moment, though, she had to be content to be worked hard and acquire exposure.

In the absence of any rational plan for making stars, 'exposure' was the commonest technique. All studios used it: but it was inevitably hit or miss. It meant putting a promising contract player into different sorts of pictures, in quick succession, usually opposite a better

48

known 'name' player of the opposite sex. But an even cheaper and sometimes more reliable form of exposure was the attention lavished on a studio hopeful by the mass-market fan magazines with voracious readers' appetites to satisfy. Publicity alone couldn't save a player whose pictures performed poorly. But a potential star could be helpfully promoted by interlocking an appealing personality, a warm public response to his or her films and a fan magazine's self-interest in 'hyping' a sympathetic success story. Davis was perfect material for interviewers: opinionated, accessible and 'different' in a way that invited the journalist to feel part of the process of presenting readers with a 'forthcoming attraction' to take the place of those whom the same writers had by now over-exposed. The laws of supply and demand, disuse and renewal, worked in her favour, and her fan interviews in these early years were some compensation for the films she had to make.

So rapidly was she shunted from one picture to another – five in her first year alone! – that she had invariably moved on to something different, and *perhaps* better, by the time the last one was released: which pleased the fans who kept faith with her by following her career.

She supported Barbara Stanwyck and George Brent in *So Big* (1932: playing an artist who fires a young man's ambition more successfully than his mother's love); Ruth Chatterton and Brent in *The Rich Are Always With Us* (1932: as an infatuated flapper girl); Warren William in *The Dark Horse* (1932: as the secretary-companion of a fast-talking, corner-cutting election agent in a political satire); Richard Barthelmess in *Cabin in the Cotton* (1932: the nymphomaniac daughter of a planter); and Warren William again in *Three on a Match* (1932: in a hand-holding 'friend in need' role).

The consistent element in this variety of subject is the concentrated exposure Davis gained from them: all were released in 1932, in April, May, June, September and October respect-

ively, testifying to the Hollywood forcing-house for talents which gossip columnists and magazine writers could transplant into their own well-manured soil. Talent-rotation and image-making were linked in turn to individual perseverance and sheer good luck. Of the former, Davis had no lack: of the latter, she had very little – and that little luck, she had to make herself.

Retrospectively, it seems a grotesque oversight on Warners' part not to recognize her potential when she played the cankered young temptress in *Cabin in the Cotton*.

Granted that her seduction scene in it stimulated laughter when the film opened on Broadway. But this was a typically 'Big City' response from the 'knowing' sophisticates. It didn't find an echo in 'the sticks', the provincial picture palaces, which was where the true fans awarded their favourites the accolade of being stars. In any case, what is risible about it is not Davis, but the awkwardness of the star she conquers. Richard Barthelmess, who went back to the days of the D. W. Griffith stock company and by 1932 was past his peak of popularity, could have held very little interest for the pitiless misogyny of the director Michael Curtiz. Curtiz, a man of brutal efficiency at work, relished the subtle sexual pathology he sometimes imposed on (or drew out of) even his routine Warner Bros assignments. The bullying techniques he sometimes employed against newcomers to see what they were made of, or even against established names to acquaint them publicly with what *he* thought they were worth, drew a defiant response from Davis. She revealed a vivid foretaste for mingling desire for a man, and at the same time contempt for him, which her later performances varied and refined. Playing Madge, the planter's spoiled child, she presents a budding specimen of a Deep South nympho, stealthily seducing the conscience-bowed sharecropper's son (Barthelmess) employed by her Daddy. Years later, she recorded her own unfavourable impressions of her leading man, an actor (she said) who exerted himself only in close-up and went totally inert in long-shot when he considered the exposure he was getting not to be worth the effort. Throughout his seduction, he wears the unhappy look of an actor who senses the scene is being 'thrown' to the supporting player. Davis's voice, a call sign pitched between a taunt and a whine, resonates with trampish selfishness. Those eyeballs prominently ogling Barthelmess from under a forehead that shines with heat like a light globe, her fingers clutching his hand as he nervously lights a cigarette for her, the flirtatious sag of her body against the shop counter, the breathy little ballad of 'Willie the Weeper' that she croons to the tune of 'Minnie the Moocher' as she strips to slip into 'something more restful', and the erotic rustle of her waist-sash being untied before she rises into the screen, bare-shouldered and presumably totally naked the rest of the way down, to call Barthelmess enticingly to his fate. Every detail adds provocation to a confidently assembled picture of a young woman in heat. The critic John Baxter scarcely exaggerates when he calls this scene 'one of the great voyeuristic experiences the cinema has afforded us.'

At the time she played this scene, Davis had just passed her twenty-fourth birthday and was still living with her mother. They made a restless pair, devoted to each other, yet living on each other's nerves. Bette was having to borrow heavily against salary. After Arliss's patronage, her career again seemed to have lost momentum. She and Ruthie had no sooner settled in one place than they began making preparations for a move to the next: it was as if each stop-over in Hollywood were a station of the cross, offering only a brief respite from some imminent martyrdom. The basis of this restlessness was in part sexual. Bette was still a sexually inexperienced girl – by her own choice. Fearful of interrupting her career by an unwanted pregnancy, she quickly disabused anyone who imagined she was 'available'. But such abstemiousness had its price. Years later,

With her first husband Harmon Nelson at the Waikiki
Club, Hollywood: his band engagements were not to bring
them so close together very often.

Sharing corn-on-the-cob with Harmon: but the marriage
was under strain from the start.

talking with Dick Cavett on television, she was
asked, 'When did you stop being a virgin?' She
recalled thinking, 'Should I be lady-like and
ignore it? Then I said, "When I was twenty-
four – and married." I knew that made me
respectable. But I added, ". . . and it was sheer
hell!"'

At the time, Ruthie and her daughter appear
to have viewed Bette's sexual continence as a
professional disorder rather than a personal
virtue. It was a 'seam in the carpet' that was
out of true, and getting more crooked with each
passing month. It had to be straightened – and
the way to do so was marriage.

She did not look very far afield: if truth be
told, she looked backwards, to a safe and
secure part of her adolescence, and chose the
young man who had filled part of it so enjoy-
ably with their shared interests in music and
play-acting. Bette's young beau Harmon Nelson had followed her to California and was
now working as a cornet player in a jazz band
that performed at the Colony Club and other
night spots. He was earning enough to propose
to her. With a speed that may have surprised
him, he was accepted. Bette Davis and he were
married, in August 1932, in neighbouring
Arizona, where the law didn't decree any
tedious waiting period between applying for
the licence and the actual wedding ceremony.
But if marriage took the pressure off Bette
Davis's self-enforced chastity, it liberated her
professional will even more fiercely. From this
time on, she seems to go into aggressive over-
drive. Of course she had more need than ever
before to throw all her considerable energy
behind her career. She now had a husband to
support, as well as a mother and a sister. Barbara was making strenuous attempts to fend
for herself. Unfortunately, this took the form
of trying to compete with her sister by looking
for jobs in the movies. It is no part of this
account to trace the sad graph of Barbara
Davis's failure to make good as an actress and
her mental decline into a form of manic depression requiring periodical mental care except to

With her younger sister Barbara ('Bobby') as children, top right, as teenagers and, below left, as star and visitor on location for *The Bride Came COD* (1941): her sister's failing health and inauspicious screen career took their toll on Bette's resources.

Below, with husband piano player and singer, Harmon Nelson, together with MGM singer, Eddie Adams at Hollywood Cirequil.

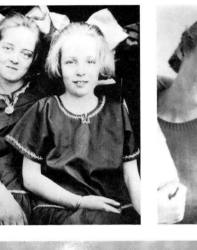

the extent that it suggests how much of Bette's energy and money had to be committed to looking after her sister until her death nearly fifty years later in 1979. In short, everything reminded Bette that she paid the bills – and thus, in the terms of the times, ruled the roost. Certainly there was a man about the house; but he was seldom about when Bette's work stopped for the day and she returned home. At that hour, Harmon was reporting for his nightclub stint with the band. It was an inversion of normal married life. At film premieres, it was her mother who acted as escort: Bette wasn't yet a big enough name to claim the arm of her current director or the male star.

Having had to shoulder obligations that usually fell on the male head of the house, she would get to the studio and spend her working day in an atmosphere dominated by men with the say-so of their superior status as producers, directors or executives. Hardly surprising that Warner Bros had now increasingly to reckon with the assertive side of a woman which had been released by marriage but not absorbed into it. She looked to her career to provide her with a sense of fulfilment – and more and more she came to interpret this in terms of her gender.

How far Katharine Hepburn's quick and apparently effortless ascent over at RKO intensified Davis's determination to succeed against the male chauvinist odds at Warner Bros must be a matter of speculation. She always admitted an admiration for her fellow Easterner, well-bred, self-confident, comfortably off, who had likewise married on an impulse and almost immediately regretted it: like Davis, she was never able to commit herself to domesticity, still less to being subordinate to a husband. Unlike Davis, her steely will and cool class-confidence had won her respect from her Hollywood studio and she had fallen on cat's feet with her first film, *A Bill of Divorcement*. Throughout 1933, Hepburn's star rose clearly and enviably in such films as *Morning Glory* and *Little Women*, the first of which won her an Academy Award as the 'Outstanding Film Actress' of that year. In the same period, Davis sweated through five Warner Bros films, playing parts that were always subservient to the male stars. The praise that the Press gave her for her labours was of the token kind: 'Does well as Fay' (*20,000 Years in Sing Sing*: with Spencer Tracy); 'Is attractive as Alabama' (*Parachute Jumper*: with Douglas Fairbanks Jr) were typical quotes, testifying to a presence, but not much chance for a performance. Even having George Arliss again as her guardian in *The Working Man* and winning the *New York Times*'s commendation for 'diction that is music to the ears' somehow lacked the rapture of their first performance together.

All the same, the exhibitors were making demands for 'more pictures with Bette Davis'. Warners couldn't ignore this news from the hinterland where the money was made. She was at least a popular talent: she *might* be star material. That was how their minds worked. The volume of the stuff written about her helped, too, since studios had a touching history of believing the very stories about their players that their own publicists had planted in 'the prints' in the first place!

So she was put into a starring role, in *Ex-Lady* (1933): but all she got out of it was status without achievement. It should not have been the embarrassment that she recalled it as being: Darryl F. Zanuck had personally selected it for her – one of his last productions before he quit Warner Bros in protest at the studio's delay in restoring the pay cuts it had forced on its staff in the cost-cutting emergency following the signs that at last the cinema box-office was being hit by the Depression. *Ex-Lady* was a remake of *Illicit*, a sex-comedy of two years earlier which owed its quite *risqué* idea that free love is preferable to betrothal to a Robert Riskin scenario. It had Robert Florey as director, with instructions to make Davis look a star. But she felt embarrassed, not enhanced, by 'smart' situations and frivolous bedroom scenes: it seemed an exercise in titillation, not

a chance to show her paces. Anyhow, even in this movie, made before the Production Code imposed its hypocritical range of 'thou shalt nots' on 'life' as Hollywood interpreted it, its thesis finally collapses in the compromise that free love may do more for the undressing scenes, but a submissive wife makes for safer box-office. It left Davis seething with dissatisfaction and despondency. 'Filmdom's Newest Favorite' was how the *Ex-Lady* poster trumpeted her below a bare-shouldered shot of her that was most displeasing. Would Hepburn have stood for *that*?

The 'favorite' was unceremoniously pitched back into the ominously titled *Bureau of Missing Persons* (1933), a potboiler that might have been a poverty-row answer to MGM's *Grand Hotel*, since 'all human life' was supposedly included in its tawdry, anecdotal but mercifully brisk account of police work. Otherwise, it had precious few star attractions, except Davis, Pat O'Brien and Lewis Stone as the ominiscient 'Chief'. She plays a woman suspected of

murdering her employer and makes little effort to hide her contempt for a part that doesn't even get her on screen until the third reel. Her eyes signal a sense of affront, as well they might after delivering a terrible passage of exposition about twin brothers and gibbering idiots that provokes Pat O'Brien to enquire of her, 'Have you been smoking hemp?'

Her sense of worth was further devalued in *Fashions of 1934* (1934), which turned her hair peroxide blonde and tried to make her into a Jean Harlow type. After that came three crime melodramas: *The Big Shakedown* (1934), *Jimmy the Gent* (1934) and the rather more interesting *Fog Over Frisco* (1934), which has remained one of her favourite films.

Directed by William Dieterle, and one of the fastest-paced mystery stories ever filmed, it offered Davis a role that might have been an audition for the 'bitch parts' she was soon to fill out in more substantial movies. She played a rich, spoilt society girl involved in crime for the sexual excitement it offers her. 'You can't

imagine the terrible thrill,' she tells her pliable fiancé whom she has implicated in a securities racket, 'wandering around with thousands of dollars right under the nose of the police.' With financial need ruled out as a redeeming motive, only sheer wanton recklessness is left – and Davis projects it with a sense of wilful release. She makes an appearance in the story the way Dietrich was to do the following year in *The Devil Is a Woman*, coming gradually into view behind a bunch of balloons in a nightclub as she bursts them one by one with her cigarette and a playgirlish cry of 'Bang! Bang!' The tics that Davis made her trademark are still in the 'patent pending' stage, but unmistakable: the 'snatch and grab' at her cigarette, the head (emphasized by swept-back blonde hair so stiffly waved as to look set in meringue) tilted boldly back to bring her eyes level with a man's, the shoulder-swinging march in a tight-assed skirt and the expletive force of a word like 'headache' that is uttered as if she is laying a curse on the irritation. Chic and deceitful, she

Below, potboiler time: *Bureau of Missing Persons* (1933) trapped her in a closet – and a dud role. Bottom left, *Jimmy the Gent* (1934), with Cagney, was scarcely better. But in *Fog Over Frisco* (1934), top, her role as a society bitch defined the features that were to be famous. Above, Warners, though, thought they had another Jean Harlow in *The Big Shakedown* (1934). *Fashions of 1934*, below, took her to the peroxided limit: she felt cheapened. Opposite, the starring role at last: but *Ex-Lady* (1933) was status without achievement.

bends men to her will by acts of what could be called financial emasculation – 'Big boy! Now write me out a cheque for $50,000.' All her broken-spirited fiancé gets out of it are four or five collusive kisses as his pen signs away his reputation – and his bank balance.

Davis finishes up dead (though her body remains unseen) in the trunk of a car with a third of the film still to run! But her heartless, amoral appeal illuminates all of it like the after-glow of a fireball.

As Nick Roddick points out in his well-researched study of the New Deal era at Warner Bros, what Davis portrays in *Fog over Frisco* is 'bad blood . . . a rotten inheritance'. And he adds, 'There is in the film . . . a tacit equation between female independence and such pathological behaviour.' True enough: but at this time any role that offered her a measure of 'independence' was welcomed by Bette Davis as relief from the accumulating frustrations of her married and professional life. If she had to be cast as an economic threat to men, this, too, was hardly surprising in a studio where the bosses were ever on the alert to the threat of an actress turning into a 'mon-ster of ingratitude' the minute she became a star. The top hierarchy at *every* Hollywood studio viewed its stars this way: hence the elaborate contract system that had come into being to control every aspect of a star's life, private, public, social and moral, in case of any misbehaviour that threatened his or her invest-ment value. Women stars were generally seen as being more 'treacherously' disposed than the male glories of the system. For one thing, *men* ran the studios; and they felt easier in their dealings with the paragons of their own sex; they knew how to talk sense into them 'man to man'; they took a more sympathetic view of any lapses in propriety, any moral 'prob-lems', since the compassionate reflection that 'There but for the grace of God . . .' was usually extended by men to men. There were also good economic reasons for this sexual favouritism. Male stars were less perishable commodities

than the females: their careers matured like good endowment policies rather than tailing off, like the female stars' frail dependence on beauty, into dwindling assets. It was unfair, of course: but when was big business based on fairness? The Warner brothers (in their flesh-and-blood lower-case reality) were business-men first and last. They resisted the blandish-ments of their women stars and claimed no *droit de seigneur* over them. Jack L. Warner had his vices; but even Davis admitted they lay outside the bedroom – presumably she referred to his gambling on the horses. In short, the view they had of their women stars corresponded to the view that wider American society took of women's place in it.

Considering all this discouragement, it's not surprising that Davis found pitiably few opportunities at first to assert herself on the screen as an independent woman. The roles she was assigned were invariably those of wives, sweethearts or employees usually described as 'loving' or 'loyal'. 'Independence' was written into the script only to the extent that it entertainingly disrupted the male-ordered world of the drama. It is unfair to ask her to take the blame for an image of womanhood that a later generation of critics represented by such able writers as Molly Haskell and Marjorie Rosen has charged with presenting the female as a continuous threat to men.

What was more important for her future was the welcome that women film-goers were giving her whenever she appeared in roles that reflec-ted the lives that many of them were leading. In her 'working girl' parts, she was constantly having to compete with men on *their* terms; and most women who still had jobs in these years knew all about that.

In *Front Page Woman* (1935) she and George Brent played crime reporters on rival tabloids. In Marjorie Rosen's words, she is 'alarmingly competent'. Each out-scoops the other, usually by foul means rather than fair, and the hard, driving pace set by Michael Curtiz propels Davis through her scenes like an animated

exclamation mark. She proves how resilient a woman has to be to survive in this world; but she cannot disguise something that is far less flattering to her sex. The price of competitiveness is a loss of femininity. The film was based on a grotesquely sexist article in the *Saturday Evening Post*; and under its original title, it was even more brutally biased than the snide gender reversal implied by the film's change of title. The article was called 'Woman Are Bum Newspapermen'. The movie awards Davis a nominal victory: she solves the crime and beats Brent to the story. But it doesn't hide its antipathy to the notion of women invading such male strongholds as the newsroom, the saloon bar and the prison (on the night of an electrocution, too: which causes her to faint dead away and have her copy filed for her by a strong-willed male like Brent). The script is peppered with scorn for her sex, from the news editor's caustic rebuke, 'You should be writing poems in birthday cards', to Brent's blunt diktat, 'If you're going to be any kind of a goat, you'll be a nanny goat and like it.' The men seem to be in a perpetual rage with her. Not because she's a woman: but because she's a woman trying to be like a man. That makes them insecure. In one scene in the bar where the newsmen gather, an unmistakably 'butch' woman journalist clad in a mannish jacket and tie, with a skirt wrapped round a pair of barrel-like limbs, is stationed in the centre of 'the boys', buying them a round of drinks. The message is clear: a woman is accepted on terms of equality only if she abandons her feminine characteristics and turns herself into a parody male.

If the memoirs of Davis and other Warner players are reliable, the atmosphere at the studio often had this feeling. It obviously wasn't in the business of turning its actresses into butch types: but it was far more satisfying to make them correspond to the male-created stereotype by playing the bitch. Not necessarily the stony-eyed Medusa with snakes in her hair: more usually the peroxide-blonded bitch who

lived by her wits and wisecracks. The work-manlike cynicism of writer and director meant that the character could always be rehabilitated for devotion and domesticity by a love affair conducted by the man with the efficiency of a snap fastener.

Despite the gutsy working girls portrayed by Davis and others, such films represented a backlash against the threatening posture of working women. Marjorie Rosen has noted the paradox that it was the *previous* decade, the 1920s, which saw the greatest recruitment of women since the First World War into jobs that placed them beside, if seldom on a par with, men. In the 1930s, when stars played secretaries, stenographers, reporters, waitresses and counter clerks, the plight of working women had actually become desperate. Ten million women were in work in 1930, according to the Department of Labor statistics; but a fifth of them would be jobless within a year or two. According to Rosen, 'Women's inalienable right to work and eat became less precious

in consideration of masculine welfare.' In short, the women were sacked as an economy measure to let the men hang on to their jobs. In Hollywood movies, too, men retained the upper hand and the studios got a lot of dramatic or comic mileage out of what women got up to in order to 'work and eat'.

Only very occasionally in these apprentice days did Davis play a working-girl role that required her to behave for reasons that had nothing to do with the 'selfish' advantage of her own sex. In *Special Agent* (1935) she was cast as a book-keeper in a shady syndicate who turns her crooked boss over to the Revenue men on patriotic grounds. Her immediate reward is to be taken out of the labour market and made the wife of the handsome investigative newsman (George Brent again!) who has exposed the racket.

A year earlier, in *Housewife* (1934), she played a successful copywriter in an advertising agency: but the prime function of this employment was simply to turn the office into a 'home from home' where her handsome employer (Brent once more!) could be enticed away from his wife by this much more competent seductress. If she lost her man, it was only because Warners weren't prepared to let the 'daytime mistress' defeat the family values represented by the absentee wife. To punish her further, she also lost her job!

The 'family' was still a sanctified institution as far as the movies were concerned: and it would continue that way until the end of the Second World War. The wiles of the single woman who saw her employer as a way to matrimony were used to keep the plot spinning: but (barring fatal accidents engineered by the writers) it was invariably the married woman who was granted custody of her floundering husband. It was a hypocrisy particularly detested by Davis. She had entered on her own marriage in the romantic belief that a strong man made for a happy wife. But her husband was proving the weaker partner; and although she's on record as yearning for him to stand up to her, knowing her nature it's doubtful if conceding the upper hand to her spouse would have given her much lasting satisfaction. Is it any wonder, therefore, that she began pursuing roles which were unflattering to the image of woman as a creature of love and generosity, but at least were devoid of the hypocrisies constituting Hollywood's vision of her sex?

She had put the pressure on Jack L. Warner ever since she had heard that RKO was planning to film Somerset Maugham's novel *Of Human Bondage*.

The idea didn't go down well with Jack L. Warner. He thought the role of an unredeemed bitch would hurt her image (and the investment she represented). There was the awesome and recent example of the harm that Joan Crawford had done herself in just such a manner. Infected by the fever to be acclaimed as a 'Great Actress' following her triumph in *Grand Hotel*, Crawford had besieged Louis B. Mayer till he loaned her out to United Artists for the role of the trashy prostitute in Maugham's *Rain*. It was a particularly attractive role to ambitious stars: Jeanne Eagels had played it on the stage and Gloria Swanson in the silent film version. But Crawford's performance revolted her fans. They called it (and, by extension, her) 'vulgar' and 'cheap'. It was too sudden a descent into raw reality. Her beloved public rebuffed her: in Crawford's eyes, they 'withdrew their love' and sent her into a temporary depression. Her popularity soon recovered; but it took much longer before she tried out another bitch role – and then she took care to preserve the glamour of bitchiness.

Maugham had based Mildred, the antiheroine of *Of Human Bondage*, on his own misogynist attitude to women and the destruction they can inflict on men. Mildred ruins a weak-willed lover out of pathological compulsion; and there was no way such a character could be reformed, humanized or rendered a victim without compromising Maugham's novel. (That consideration didn't always deter Hollywood, of course: but Warner knew he wouldn't get the profit of a successful bowdlerization, so why take the blame for it?) He said No to Davis – but the only effect was to redouble her pleading. His obstructiveness was met with her relentlessness. He grew disturbed by her degree of desperation.

It is unlikely that he guessed one possible reason for what he saw as her rush to self-destruction. Towards the end of 1933, Davis found herself expecting her first child. It should have been happy news for husband and wife. Instead, the appearance of a baby would interrupt her career at a crucial stage; and because she would have to go on suspension without pay, it would add a crushing burden to the household bills that her husband's inferior income couldn't meet by itself. Both Harmon and Ruthie urged her not to have the baby; and, for once, she did what she was told – and bitterly regretted it for years. Her health suffered: so did her marriage. The open disdain in which she now held her husband probably derived from the self-reproach she felt for sacrificing herself to him this once. More than ever, work was her only catharsis.

Her next film provided an outlet for her pent-up feelings – and it did more. *Bordertown* (1935) both released her anger and allowed her simultaneously to rehearse the role of a driven and vindictive woman for the part which she really craved to play in *Of Human Bondage*.

Bordertown cast Paul Muni, an actor with a sympathetic bent for playing underdogs, as a poor but dedicated Mexican lawyer whose faith in all things American is shaken by the racial prejudice he meets. Denied success and self-respect, he heads back to a boom-town on the US-Mexican border determined to grab all he can get – and, of course, getting more than he bargained for. Davis, beaded, braceleted and befurred, is the seedy casino owner's tramp of a wife who makes an immediate play for Muni when he's hired as the bar-room bouncer and, to make room for him in her bed, kills her husband. Her seductive allure seems kindled out of the same garish glow that Tony Gaudio's photography casts over the harshly lit club.

Davis could already fashion a character's motivation out of her own frustration more forcefully than the writers could plant it in the script; and here, her vituperative spray of contempt for a lover she perceives to be weaker than herself converts infatuation into contempt. 'If it wasn't for me, you'd still be rolling drunks at the Silver Slipper. I made you rich. I put those swell clothes on your back. Now just because you got your neck washed, you think you're a gentleman. No one can make you that – you're riff-raff. And so am I. You belong to me, and you're going to stay with me because I'm holding on to you. I committed murder to get you.'

With the same force, she won her point in an argument with director Archie Mayo about the way her 'mad' scene should be played in court. He wanted histrionics: she gave him realism, eschewing the Bedlam gesturing in favour of a chilling glaze on those prominent eyeballs that stared ahead to another, more 'up-market' mad scene she would play as the Empress Carlotta of Mexico in *Juarez* (1939), another film she made with Muni some five years later.

Throughout shooting, she nagged on about *Of Human Bondage*. Whether Jack L. Warner sued for peace or whether he actually did say, 'Let her go hang herself,' is unclear: but he finally gave in. One reason, however, may have had to do with the business deal it facilitated. Warner Bros owned the film rights to the Rodgers and Hammerstein musical *Sweet Adeline* and badly wanted Irene Dunne for it: but RKO had her under contract. So Davis was exchanged for Dunne.... Maybe Warner thought that if Davis was hell-bent on committing professional suicide by playing a cheap trollop like Mildred, it was best she did it at someone else's expense in *their* studio.

Though she had completed *Bordertown* before beginning *Of Human Bondage*, it wasn't

67

premiered till six months after the nation had absorbed the shock of what Davis did to herself in the latter movie.

For her, *Of Human Bondage* has remained a landmark. She pushed her characterization of Mildred, Maugham's devouring woman who feeds on Leslie Howard's limply acquiescent medical student, to the point of masochism. Perc Westmore, the make-up expert, had begun accentuating her dominant characteristics as early as 1931 when he turned her heart-shaped memento of a flapper girl's lips into a horizontal line by applying lipstick with a bolder stroke. Her mouth ceased to look bee-stung: it became a cutlass slash. Now the brilliant costume designer Walter Plunkett put together a wardrobe for Mildred that looked a parody of cheap femininity: polka-dot dresses and ruffles snaking provocatively around the bosom. In contrast, the waitress's uniform she wears has a hint of the emblematic costume of 'domination' rites. As consumption begins to devour Mildred, Davis herself applied the ravishing physical symptoms of her decline and punishment with a hand that got heavier and heavier. By her final scenes, the impression is not of medical verisimilitude, but self-mutilation. Maybe she recalled how, as a burnt child, people's sympathy for her had faded as the bandages came off. In *Of Human Bondage*, she held their interest by intensifying an audience's fascination with the extent of the psychic damage this wretched woman inflicts on herself and others.

She invited a London Cockney girl to come and live with her and her family in their already cramped home for several weeks before shooting began, so that she could absorb the right accent for Mildred. That accent remains one of the most striking things in the film. 'Mildred's whining, snarling, shrewish tones have never left this actress's linguistic manners,'

Opposite, the landmark role: as the devouring Mildred who feeds on Leslie Howard's masochistic hero in *Of Human Bondage* (1934). Below, a hint of 'domination' in her waitress's uniform in *Of Human Bondage*.

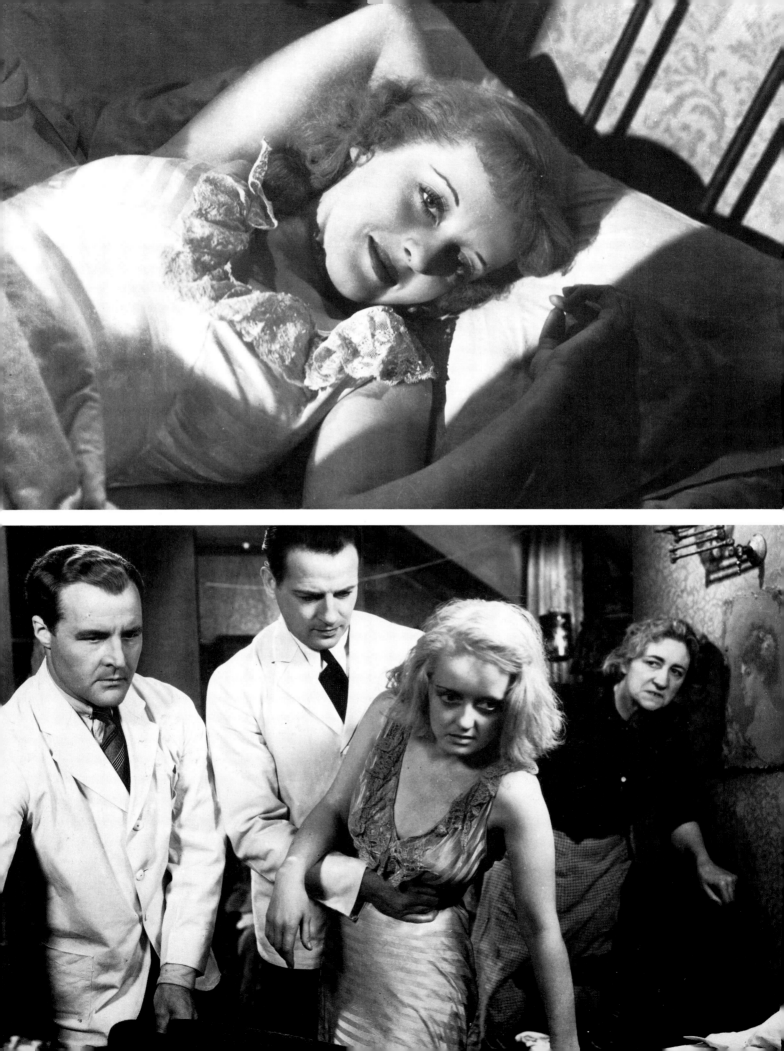

wrote the American critic Parker Tyler. '[She] exemplifies the sarcastic woman, the legendary cat of colloquial esteem, and her roles are selected to utilize the native quality of her voice, which, even in its pleasant moods, secretes those cynical harmonies that express a sophisticated, neurotic, artificial kind of femininity.' Graham Greene characterized her 'disturbing talent' in *Of Human Bondage* as 'wickedly good – up to a point, the point where passion got a little tattered' and registered with fascination 'that precise nervy voice, the pale ash-blonde hair, the popping neurotic eyes, a kind of corrupt and phosphorescent prettiness.'

Davis herself has recalled that Mildred's reality emerged 'as immediate as a newsreel'. If the very power of her performance severely unbalances the film, it remains a monstrous exercise in character creation the like of which Hollywood was not to see again until Marlon Brando imported the Method style in the 1950s. Davis reached the same end as Brando by comparable means. For inspiration, she drew on her own unsatisfactory marriage to a man whom she alternately willed to stand up to her, then reviled for failing to do so. In the face of her vituperative taunting, the polite acting conventions of Leslie Howard seem to belong in another film. To adapt Kenneth Tynan's verdict on Brando, that 'he doesn't mind bruising his soul', one could say that Davis takes an active delight in bruising her mind, body and soul. Like Brando, her own long-term relationship with the movies was to be one of creative belligerency. Both believed that in order to act, one had to 'upset oneself'. In *Of Human Bondage*, for the first time, Davis provided evidence of just how powerful an 'upset' she was capable. Interviewed for *Modern Screen* shortly after the film's premiere, she revealed how much had been riding on it. 'Mother and Ham [her husband] drove home from the preview at Santa Barbara. I didn't go. I was afraid to go because the reaction meant so much to me. I didn't sleep naturally. I lay awake, every nerve tense.

I worked myself into a lather. . . . The hours crawled. At last the front door opened, and they came in quietly. I hadn't expected that. I crept down the stairs and looked at them. They looked at me. Their faces were blank. They didn't say a word.' Even the Warner Bros people were impressed – 'stunned' would be no exaggeration – but unwilling to second-guess the public's reaction. The fact that *Of Human Bondage* proved a box-office disappointment did not cancel out the scale of Davis's ambition and achievement. Her full-length portrait of female malevolence separated itself so completely from issues of commercial success or failure that it became a talking point even among people who had decided such a film was much too 'unpleasant' for them to see

In short, she achieved *on film* the kind of impact that her short-lived stage career had been leading up to in New York. Her Mildred was film acting charged with the elemental vigour of the theatre. The public tends to hoard one or two special films in its collective memory, and it is these that become the basis of a star's image. Davis wrought her image so fiercely in *Of Human Bondage* that for years afterwards she kept meeting people who believed it was her *first* picture, even though there had been twenty-one before it.

Film-goers actually did – and still do – associate a star with the character that he or she plays: it's at the interface of the two that the phenomenon of stardom takes shape. But Bette Davis's hold over her public isn't to be explained by such a naïve, such a libellous equation. A lot of her power came from the way her will to take command interacted so completely with the character she was playing that she was taken over by it; but part also comes from the feelings she invoked in the women who longed to take command to the same degree. Her rage, according to Marjorie Rosen, represented the submerged fury of every woman who had ever felt powerless in love, marriage or life. 'How easy for women to watch Bette vent frustration for them and

then nod: "What a lousy broad." How comforting for men to see that female strength implied lack of scruple. And how sensational!'

Now the brakes were off . . . and a few months later, back at Warner Bros, she created another memorable bitch in Joyce Heath, the alcoholic actress on the skids at the start of *Dangerous* (1936) who attracts men and destroys them without ever falling into anything resembling conventional love. What Joyce is in love with is the power drive: a man is only an adjacent object for it to fasten on to. Desire isn't absent: but the minute the man surrenders to her, it is replaced by contempt. Rescued from dipsomania by Franchot Tone and put back on to the stage in a play he has financed himself, her rehabilitation is as unacceptable to her as respectability would be. She must reject it. So she deliberately steers her car into a tree, hoping to kill her discarded husband for refusing her a divorce. She survives, as intended: but he is only crippled. This kind of situation, where the man has been reduced to a dependent object, always made a strong dramatic appeal to Davis. For several decades, as various times, she tried to set up a production of *Ethan Frome*, the Edith Wharton novel which has just such a situation as its centrepiece. (Later, much later, she derived a certain compensation from having a paraplegic Joan Crawford at her mercy in *What Ever Happened to Baby Jane?*)

But sheer evil is not what Davis incarnates, although the English critic E. Arnott Robinson once commented: 'I think Bette Davis would probably have been burned as a witch had she lived two or three hundred years ago. She gives the curious feeling of being charged with power which can find no ordinary outlet.' What keeps characters like Mildred and Joyce hacking their way through a veritable forest of absurdities that a less 'charged' actress than Davis would have clipped away at impotently with manicure scissors is the fact that they are unhindered by the least sense of the consequence of their actions. Temperaments like this

flourish in the world of theatre and cinema. They impose their own vacuum on all around them until normality, like Nature, rushes in to fill it with a 'happy ending' or a horrid comeuppance. Franchot Tone has this redeeming function, despite Davis's sneering, nagging, betraying and almost ruining him. Indifference to guilt is Joyce Heath's jinx and a large part of Davis's 'presence'. She never asks for pity, understanding or compassion: it is enough to pull others into her neurosis. In one scene in *Dangerous*, she and Tone take shelter from a storm in a hay-filled barn. The air is charged with emotional static. Tone responds to a gesture that she leaves ambiguously inviting; and a tiny crooked smile of entrapment flickers for a second or two across her face without his observing it. It is the most intimate moment of collusion between her and her audience that she had achieved up to then.

Davis had hoped her performance in *Of Human Bondage* would win her a 1934 Academy Award. Warner Bros, always alive to the

Left, with Victor McLaglen at the 1936 Academy Awards. *Dangerous* **won her the first of her two Oscars.**

Looking soulful, right, (but really suffering from dust and boredom) as Gaby the waitress who reads Villon in the appositely named *The Petrified Forest* **(1936).**

To put life into a dull moment, pull a gun. Davis and Howard find chaste love no match for Bogart's existentialist act. Even love under the giant cacti somehow lacks the grand passion.

chance of saving money and aware that RKO would collect a large part of the profit of any voting campaign mounted around Davis, released her earlier film *Bordertown* one month before the Academy ceremony and tried to attract some of the praise their star received for *Of Human Bondage* towards their own studio's production. But the Best Actress award went to Claudette Colbert for *It Happened One Night*, in which, ironically, Frank Capra had wanted Davis for the role of the spoilt-brat heroine. The *New York Times* commented: 'While Miss Davis won substantial support, she did not in the least jeopardize Miss Colbert.' By 1936, things were very different. On 5 March that year, Davis won the coveted statuette for *Dangerous*; and as the Academy's voting methods allowed preferences to be publicly expressed at that period, it was recorded that she won it by a large margin over Katharine Hepburn (the second choice, for *Alice Adams*) and Elisabeth Bergner (the third choice, for *Escape Me Never*). At that time,

Davis was not even an Academy member! Warner Bros had again released a new film of hers, *The Petrified Forest* (1936), a month before the awards; and RKO, wise to the same voting strategy, released Hepburn's new movie, *Sylvia Scarlett*, a full *two* months earlier! It was always believed by Davis that the award was actually accorded her for *Of Human Bondage*: possibly it was a case of delayed shock!

The Petrified Forest hasn't stood the ravages of time. Piously adapted from Robert E. Sherwood's success of the 1935 Broadway season, its characters are the fixtures and transients of a filling-station-cum-diner on the edge of the Arizona flat lands and they engage interminably in the sort of matinée philosophizing that passed for seriousness in its day and with its middle-brow audience. In intention, a sort of *Outward Bound* (which Warners had produced in 1930), its ennui tempts one to rename it *Nowhere Bound*. It undercut from the start Davis's power to impose herself on unlikely

75

Opposite, still at the studio's beck and call: a publicity shot in the projection box couldn't hide her distaste for such chores.

Left, *The Golden Arrow* **(1936) with George Brent: a film begun under protest and finished by capitulation.**

material by casting her as one of the half-dozen spiritual waifs and sentimentalized strays who hold forth on life and death, and seemingly all the halts in between, with undramatized loquacity. She plays Gaby, the waitress who reads François Villon and yearns to learn about art and beauty, especially if she can take the course in Paris, France, since 'the French seem to understand everything'. She was again co-starred with Leslie Howard (brought over from the Broadway production) as the wistful hobo, an idealist defeated by experience, who arranges his own death in the end so that the insurance policy – on which he has surprisingly kept the premiums up to date – shall finance Gaby's travelling scholarship.

Davis's pretence at vulnerability appears as forced as her eager girlishness. That nasal whine, such a powerful motor to propel her through her bitch roles, is modulated into a pseudo-poetic breathiness – the equivalent of someone putting on an accent to go with a higher class of goods. She might have done

better to be a tougher babe: only Monroe learned the trick of making Tolstoy her guide and protector. But part of the trouble is that Davis has no one to react to. Howard is too soft, too intent on playing to *his* sort of audience. For all his self-conscious 'tenderness', he patronizes her. And Humphrey Bogart, as Duke Mantee, the gangster on the run who acts on impulse, is an existentialist age away from everyone else in the film. He alone manages to kick it into occasional life.

Davis was awarded some compliments that appear a little backhanded. Typical of them was Frank Nugent's in the *New York Times*: '[She] demonstrates that she does not have to be hysterical to be credited with a grand portrayal.'

Making the film was a wretched experience. Though it looks as if it has been made entirely in a studio, Archie Mayo took the cast and crew to Arizona for the establishing scenes, and the heat, wind and dust seared Davis's tender skin, enflamed her eyes and blocked her sinuses. The fuller's earth blown over the set by wind machines back in the studio to reproduce the desert atmosphere laid her up with aggravated headaches. Twenty-nine films in five years were starting to take their toll of her health. The Oscar award, which she rose from her sick bed to receive, didn't mollify her: it simply symbolized an integrity that she had to defend.

Jack L. Warner was wearily familiar with such danger signs. The reaction to the congratulatory telegram was often ingratitude – or so he saw it. For his star, an Oscar was a status symbol which entitled her to 'worthy' roles: for him, it was a commercial token that had to be exchanged for what his star was worth at the box-office. Quite soon, in fact, he would be asked what Davis *was* worth to him; and it is instructive to know that at this stage, according to the head of Warner Bros, 'Any film of ours in which (Bette Davis) appears is worth $600,000 to $700,000 gross in the world' *Any* film, please note, irrespective of merit. Davis might argue (and did, we may be sure) that she and the studio had a mutual interest in making pictures commensurate with her importance; but Warner had a vested interest in not allowing a star's ego to be the grit that fouled up the production machine.

Health problems, money worries, prestige anxieties: such were the elements in the confrontation scenes between her and Warner in the spring and summer of 1936. To get away from it all, she took a trip to New York, intending to attend the Democratic National Convention as friend and supporter of President Roosevelt, whom she admired because his party was committed to the idea of an American National Theatre. No sooner had she got to New York, than a cable arrived instructing her to report back to the studio for a retake in a screwball comedy, *The Golden Arrow* (1936), that she had made under protest in the first place. The director had thought up a new wheeze: he wanted a scene showing her and co-star George Brent with black eyes! After angry exchanges, she capitulated and arrived back in Hollywood in a state of nervous exhaustion. Almost immediately she was lumbered with a script called *God's Country and the Woman*. She was to play a timber boss: the title already suggested the burden she would have to carry. She turned it down flat. Her rejection soon blew up into a first-class row over her contract. Warners offered her a new seven-year one, at $2,000 a week rising to $4,000 (still a couple of thousand dollars below what a crony of Jack L. Warner like Errol Flynn received). She held out for $3,000 to start with, a two-year contract, six weeks paid vacation and parts worthy of her – if need be, parts in movies made for other studios. Warner raged. She was 'arbitrary and obstinate'. He placed her on suspension.

Every one of her co-players had suffered the same humiliations, and they monitored the battle eagerly. One notable resistance leader was Jimmy Cagney. Cocky and high-tempered, he would confront his boss, insult Warner in the yiddish swear words he knew and threaten to throw up his film career and go to medical school to become a doctor. Joan Blondell later recalled, 'Cagney was a big fighter and he used to say to me I should just get up and walk out. "That's all you have to do, and then you'll get what you want and get some good part."' At the very moment when Davis and Warner were locked in acrimony, Cagney found his contract had been broken on the technical point of Pat O'Brien's name being billed above his own in one of his films. He abruptly quit Warner Bros, signed up with an independent company and, pending the outcome of the suit Warners filed against him, proceeded to make two films. A tired and frustrated Davis may well have had her next move triggered by Cagney's example – for, after all, the fact that his action was deemed unlawful wouldn't be known for a year or so.

Leaving her mother and sister in the care of her business manager, with enough money set aside to pay the rent that Cecil B. DeMille charged them for the house they were living in, she flew to Canada, then took the train and boat to England.

To have two of his stars defect at the same moment seemed to Warner like organized rebellion. Moreover, Davis soon made it plain she didn't intend to sit it out in idleness. She already had two films lined up for her in England.

Her plans are usually referred to vaguely in the accounts of this episode: one is left to assume that because the man who said he was going to produce the films, one Ludovico Toeplitz, had an obscure history and made himself scarce when the drama reached the law courts rather than the film studio, the projects had little substance. This is untrue. Toeplitz de Grand Ry, to give him his full name, was Italian (not Polish, as is usually stated), a financier who had funded several of Alexander Korda's early films including *The Private Life of Henry VIII*. His lawyer was Filippo Del Guidice, who also had ambitions to be a pro-

The 'naughty young lady' just before losing in the action Warners brought against her in the English High Court in 1936.

ducer, and in fact was to go on and produce some of the best British films between 1939 and 1958 including Olivier's *Henry V* and *Hamlet*. To put under contract Bette Davis, an Oscar winner and international star, would mean world-wide sales for any of her films produced by these people in Britain. Two were already lined up for her: the first, *I'll Take the Low Road*, to be directed by another Italian, Monte Banks, then Gracie Fields' husband; the second, a project to co-star Maurice Chevalier. No wonder Jack L. Warner and his lawyers came in hot pursuit: this was more than a star's temperamental fugue.

Davis was promptly sued in the English High Courts for breach of contract. Clause 23 of a twenty-page contract, referred to sarcastically by her Counsel as 'the whole collective memory of mankind', stated if she failed, refused or neglected to perform her services, her employers had the right 'to extend the term of this agreement and all of its provisions for a period equivalent to the period during which such failure, refusal or neglect shall be continued.' As reported in the London *Times*, Counsel for Davis, Sir William Jowitt, declared that if she walked out of a film 'the specified period (of her contract) . . . could never come to an end at all. The bar against Miss Davis working for anyone else would never come to an end, either. It is a life sentence.' This was almost the only legal point at issue; and, unfortunately for Davis, these were almost the only words with any relevance to the issue that Sir William addressed to Mr Justice Lewis. He had a feeble grasp of the realities of life and work in Hollywood. In cross-examination of Jack L. Warner, he missed the point again and again and was rebutted by Warner's cocksure responses.

Counsel for the plaintiff, Sir Patrick Hastings, a noted playwright as well as barrister, outwitted Jowitt as if he had written his own lines to cap the other's. He opened with a description of Davis calculated to catch the headlines in every paper the next day and cut her down to size. 'I can't help but think, M'Lud,' he began, 'this is the action of a very naughty young lady.' At once, Davis ceased to look like a proud lioness defending her right to the jungle and became a spoilt kitten mewing for more milk – or, as her memoirs put it, 'an intractable infant who needed a good spanking.'

Sir Patrick's remark actually contained more irony that anyone admitted at the time. For the role of the 'naughty young lady' in which Warners had cast their artist so as to make an example of her hardly differed in essentials from many of the screen roles in which they had made a star of her. A 'good spanking' is maybe too light a retribution for the damage done by some of her screen bitches; but otherwise, the epithets 'greedy', 'high-handed' and 'spoiled', which were bandied about in the Law Courts, apply perfectly to the roles she had played in *Cabin in the Cotton*, *Fog Over Frisco*, *Of Human Bondage* and *Dangerous*. When it came to protecting their own financial invest-ment, Warners had a pretty shrewd idea of casting: only in the matter of satisfying their stars' artistic aspirations did they prove to be slow learners.

The studio won, of course. Warners were granted a three-year injunction (or the dura-tion of her contract: whichever were the longer) restraining Davis from working for anyone but them. She had to pay their costs as well as her own: a bill of some $100,000 (or £20,000). She was left dispirited – and almost broke.

In spite of everything, her Yankee backbone refused to let her proud neck bow to the inevit-able and she was contemplating going to the Court of Appeal when her old benefactor George Arliss (then sixty-eight, but fresh from his third film that year!) advised her to 'rise above defeat. ... Go back and face them proudly.' She took his paternal advice and went back. Arliss, for the last time, had played God to her.

4

CONQUEST

JACK L. WARNER WAS A HARD TASKMASTER; BUT he was not a man to bear a grudge. Especially if he had come out of a fight looking like the winner. There could be no doubt about that. The legal action (which Davis had to pay for, despite publicity releases suggesting Warners would be chivalrous as well as victorious and meet her bill as well as their own) had confirmed Warner's cast-iron contract system. But it had also confirmed Davis's image as a woman who would do battle for her rights. Honour was satisfied; what was now necessary for both parties was profit.

That, too, was soon satisfied. On her return to Hollywood, she was rushed into *Marked Woman* (1937) and it was shot, completed and released in under fourteen weeks.

Based on a published series of interviews with penitent prostitutes whose evidence had helped convict Charles 'Lucky' Luciano in 1936, thereby boosting the political career of the prosecuting DA, Thomas E. Dewey, the film presented Davis with a role that dramatized a hot social issue – and thereby gained an importance for her that pure fiction wouldn't have done. As one of 'the girls', tactfully bowdlerized from being whores in a brothel to hostesses in a clip-joint but leaving little doubt about their real business, she looks after her own interests at first; then, on the rebound from her kid sister's death at the hands of the vice king, turns revenger and finally reformer. A shrewdly written role: she could first play against its moral bias, then along with it. She starts out as a 'loner', talking tough, killing her own feelings because, well, the economics of the trade demand it: 'Some of us will end up with the short ends, but not me, baby. I know all the angles and I think I'm smart enough to keep one step ahead of them – until I get enough to pack it all in and live on easy street the rest of my life. I know how to beat this racket.' Her sister's violent death persuades her otherwise: then a double cross is carved on her face, as a warning to keep her mouth shut. Davis had her own doctor

bandage her 'injuries' professionally – and so well that Hal Wallis, head of production, briefly imagined she had had a real accident when she returned trussed up to the studio.

Though sentimental in much of its story, *Marked Woman* is remarkable for the honesty of feeling that Davis summons to the scene round her hospital bed when she pleads with the other girls to join her in testifying against the racketeer. Instead of a single woman making her commitment to civic virtue while in a man's embrace, she successfully conducts one of the rare scenes of consciousness-raising among her own sex that a Hollywood film had shown up to then. At the end of the movie, when the women have testified in a tense courtroom scene, the camera cuts Davis out of the pack as she walks off alone into the fog – Humphrey Bogart's character of the DA is too obviously based on Thomas Dewey to permit him to walk after her. The effect is to isolate her and dignify her as Woman – lonely but capitalized. The other women go their separate ways, too: but, for a moment, group loyalty has been affirmed. *Marked Woman* is a feminist film of some power and deserves respect, even though the power that appealed to Warner Bros was a hot story out of the headlines.

The three films that followed it, all released (in May, September and November 1937) like rapid-fire bullets, all display Hal Wallis's technique of offering a 'Bette Davis' for all kinds of film-goers. Where a star today who changes style makes an almost epochal event out of it, it's salutary to remember that rotation through the genres was simply part of good management under the studio system.

In *Kid Galahad*, she was simply a loyal broad in a man's world of boxing: but at least she looked to be there by choice, not necessity; in *That Certain Woman* she was a woman with a past (and a baby). But this remake of Gloria Swanson's successful first talkie, *The Trespasser*, was more than bearable because of Edmund Goulding who directed it and, being English and a favourite director of Garbo's,

With Bogart in *Marked Woman* (1937): despite the persuasion of a man's embrace, her hooker made her commitment to civic virtue out of solidarity with her own sex.

Below, with Edward G. Robinson as a loyal broad in *Kid Galahad* (1937) . . . and as a woman with a past (and a baby) who put Henry Fonda in her present in *That Certain Woman* (1937).

And Warners, letting no anniversary pass that could yield a publicity shot, celebrate her 28th birthday with a two-foot by ten-inch cake. Guests included her co-star (Henry Fonda), director (Edmund Goulding) and cameraman (Ernest Haller).

had flattering credentials as well as a reputation for being a good 'woman's director'. His homosexual temperament gave him a feminine affinity with several of the best-known women stars. Unlike Michael Curtiz, his care in enhancing their feminine side got results – *and* their gratitude. 'He concentrated on attractive shots of me,' Davis later recorded in her commentary to the book *Mother Goddam*. 'In other words, gave me the star treatment. It was the first time I had had this. I was always a member of the cast – a leading member – but not special in the way Goulding made me special in this film. *And* in the last scene, in chiffon, a large beautiful picture hat, and a glamorous hair-do, I looked *really* like a "movie star".'

But it is the last of this trio of films that shows a facet of Davis hitherto restricted to the flip comebacks that the molls, mistresses and career girls she played had stored in their mouth like chewing-gum. *It's Love I'm After* displayed a comic Davis.

85

Opposite, with Leslie Howard in *It's Love I'm After* (1937) as a Broadway couple like the Lunts who are the best of enemies on and off stage: his practice piece for *Pygmalion*, hers for *All About Eve*.

Below, friends and relations: visiting Gary Cooper on the set of *Sergeant York* . . . and making decisions with her long-time stand-in Sally Sage during shooting on *Kid Galahad*.

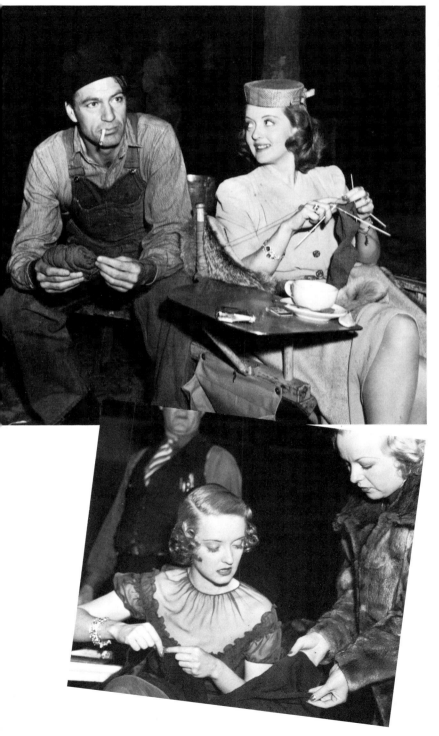

Leslie Howard again partnered her, both of them playing a couple of egotistical Broadway stars resembling the Lunts in their premarital days, striking quips off each other like matches in a Casey Robinson screenplay that has kept its own powder dry all these years.

As Davis and Howard were not the best of friends off screen, there is the added relish of seeing them play the best of enemies on it. They open it as a Romeo and Juliet chewing each other up *sotto voce* as they play the death scene. 'Your Juliet's here, my pet, not up in that box,' hisses Davis, tugging her Romeo's attention from the love-struck heiress (Olivia de Havilland) whose infatuation for him he is later hired to cure by putting on a spectacular display of boorishness at her parents' Pasadena mansion. He growls back, 'Take your hand away from my face – they can't see me.' Their spat continues off-stage and all through New Year's Eve. Self-parody, to be sure; but each raps out a certain truth about the conceit that goes with their trade. They display that total disregard for anyone else's feelings or convenience that's essential in screwball comedy. Howard was to play the acerbic Professor Higgins in the British film of *Pygmalion* the next year: his performance in *It's Love I'm After* resembles a practice sketch. And in years to come, Davis was to play another *monstre sacré* in *All About Eve*. It's as if she is already tuning up for that full-bodied concerto in star wilfulness. Together, they strike up a perfect *folie à deux* in the comic key. As Howard does his worst to make the girl fall out of love with him, Davis does her best to stop the girl's father making a pass at her. 'Wouldn't it be amusing,' she snaps at her co-star, 'if I came back as your mother-in-law?' And for a joyous moment, pure lunacy reigns. It is extraordinary that this comedy has never been remade. It is also just as well: which of today's stars would threaten to permutate their relationship into that of 'in-laws' the way Davis does to Howard and make it appear as if an antic curse had come home to roost?

What stills photographer could resist the period look of a crinoline?

By late 1937, Davis's first marriage was on the rocks. Poor Ham Nelson! the 'Hollywood wife', shut out of her famous husband's myth, was the convention of the times: the 'Hollywood husband' of the 1930s filled the man who played the part with the sort of resentment common to the women who sought their own liberation in later times.

As for Davis, work was no longer even the catharsis it had been: simply the extention of her temperament. *Jezebel* (1938) permanently annealed that temperament.

Jezebel has many times been compared with *Gone With the Wind*, which appeared twenty months later, but whose long gestation period gave Warners ample opportunity for 'comparison', at least, while shooting their own American Civil War film. According to David O. Selznick, *Gone With the Wind*'s producer, Davis was actually referred to as 'Scarlett' while *Jezebel* was in the making. But as narrative, it compares poorly. Yellow fever, its big set-piece, can't hold a candle to the panorama of Atlanta on fire. And the ending, with the heroine going off to a leper colony to nurse the man she loves, comes as anti-climax, not crescendo. The mover and shaker of events is not the plot: it is the heroine figure of its generic title, and that figure is Davis, barely needing to have her own temperament refracted dramatically through the character of Julie Marsden, the reckless belle who goes after life amidst an avalanche of conventions precipitated by her misbehaviour.

Warner Bros had bought the stage play as early as 1935. Ironically, its star had been Davis's once and future nemesis, Miriam Hopkins. The studio saw its potential – and its drawbacks. 'It is not very good,' a story department executive's memo to Hal Wallis records, 'but it could provide a good role for Bette Davis who can knock spots off a little bitch of an aristocratic Southern girl.' Naturally enough, Miriam Hopkins felt she should have first go at the spot-knocking contest: but she was bought off with a half-promise that

Warners can have had little intention of honouring. But no sooner had the studio got the property than Jack L. Warner discovered that his star was walking out on her contract. He tried holding her back by telling her that David O. Selznick was considering her for a role in the film version of a new novel which Selznick had purchased in the galley stage. The novel was *Gone With the Wind*; the role, that of Scarlett O'Hara. 'I bet it's a pip,' she spat out – as she left. It was one of those great mistakes of history that most stars make sometime or other.

Thus *Jezebel* offered both consolation for Davis and competition to Selznick; for it ended its unusually lengthy three-month shooting schedule just as Selznick's well-publicized search for a Scarlett O'Hara reached its climax. He had, of course, considered Davis; and Warner would have lent her out (and Errol Flynn as Rhett Butler: much to Davis's distaste) provided he could distribute this independent production. But Selznick was already committed to an MGM release. What kind of Scarlett she would have made must remain speculative: but probably a much stronger one than Vivien Leigh presented – a vixen to the English actress's minx. She might thus have seriously unbalanced the movie. Gable's male chauvinism gets off unscathed with a condescending 'Frankly, my dear, I don't give a damn'; it's not so certain that he wouldn't have given a damn if Davis, not Leigh, had been handing it out.

For once, in *Jezebel*, Davis had been granted a director who behaved to her the way she had wanted her husband to behave (in theory, anyhow). William Wyler was able to give orders and see them obeyed. In him, Davis confessed, 'I'd met my match.' Wyler was German by birth – Carl Laemmle, who had given him his Hollywood start at Universal, was a distant cousin – and his family had Swiss roots, too. Later that year he married Margaret Tallichet, a film actress whose family, like Davis's, was of Huguenot descent. He and Davis had thus an affinity from the start: indeed he is generally believed to be the unidentified person in her memoirs whom she called the only man to master her, and more than one tongue has spoken of an 'affair' which would have led to marriage had one or other, fearing a strong match would mean a weaker partner, not withdrawn. Of course she had profited from 'strong' directors before: Michael Curtiz, for example. But Curtiz got what he wanted by wearing down the resistance; Wyler obtained perfection by demanding dedication. The end was excellence; the education was painful; but pupils prepared to submit to it never forgot the lesson. Arliss had taught Davis continuity: Wyler taught her control. One of his memos in the Warner archives, addressed to Hal Wallis and Henry Blanke (the film's production supervisor), reads: '[Davis] comes in . . . eager to do it right, maybe overdo it . . . And I tell her to take it easy . . . Not every scene [is important], so she learns not to act everything at the same pressure, as though her life depended on it.'

All the same, seldom is any heroine's inner nature so immediately defined as Davis's in *Jezebel*. It's as if life, liberty and the pursuit of men *did* depend upon it! Late for her own party, since she scorns the dull virtue of punctuality, she gallops up to the family mansion on a horse whose own restlessness represents its mistress's. As she strides into the reception room, she whips her long riding habit into step with her, subduing its crackling folds with her riding crop: one feels she would whip horseflesh the same way, or even human flesh. Wyler reportedly put her through that single gesture thirty times over – he was master of the notion that detail is character. Like her spirited steed, the red dress that Julie elects to wear to the chaste town ball signifies her scorn of convention, her sexual recklessness. This time Wyler places his camera practically on the floor, so that the swirling crinoline's dark mass draws nigh and recedes like a thunder cloud on the shocked horizon of the conventionally white-clad dancers. The film is not in colour: but

Wyler charges the dress's black tones with such shock value that it might well be. Her reluctant partner is Henry Fonda, and his stiff arm seems to be holding a dagger between Davis's shoulder blades as he presses home her self-inflicted humiliation by insisting on their continuing to dance when a temporary loss of nerve impels her to retire in confusion. For his insolence, she slaps his face – then promises herself, 'He'll be back.' 'After *Jezebel*,' wrote one film critic, 'Scarlett herself should have no terrors.'

Davis portrays a woman whose real aim is not love, but power, superiority, conquest. Julie pays the same romantic lip-service as Davis herself did to the notion of a woman humbling herself before her man. But no sooner has this man re-entered her life with a wife in tow than Julie reverts with some relief to battle tactics: 'I've got to think, to plan, to fight. If I can't have him. . . .' In short, possession is nine-tenths of passion. Julie is just too pragmatic a person to be a truly fateful victim:

she engineers disasters, including her best friend's in a provoked duel. Unlike a Garbo character, she is not a passive woman of mystery: unlike a Dietrich *femme fatale*, she is not a siren on whose rock of disdain men dash themselves to death. Davis turns mystique into energy – and the women in the audience could enjoy the perversity of her conduct even more because historical distance separated this Jezebel from modern models of malevolence.

Even so, Warners didn't risk an unregenerate Julie. The plague that nearly finishes off Fonda provides her with the chance to plead her case with his wife that if anyone is to nurse him on the island where infected victims are isolated it should be she – his mistress. One can take this as a final surrender to decency. Or one can take it as the final effrontery of a woman out to supplant the wife rather than succour the husband. The likelihood is that contemporary audiences, cued by Warner Bros' celestial choir, left the cinema granting Bette the privilege of a purer love than a married woman

William Wyler rehearses Fonda and Davis in the *piece de scandale* in *Jezebel*, where her red dress . . . clashes with the ball's conventions and the town's proprieties.

could give. (Oddly, though Davis's memoirs recall Wyler's camera focusing on the wedding ring worn by the actress playing Fonda's wife as a symbol of her claim to possession of her husband, this close-up doesn't appear in the released print: by its absence, the balance of sympathy is further tilted Davis's way.)

On 12 February 1939, by the votes of twelve thousand members of the film industry, Bette Davis was acclaimed Best Actress for her work in *Jezebel* – and so won her second Oscar.

As if to throw Julie into starker relief, Warners had, four months before the vote, released *The Sisters* (1938), the film Davis had made immediately after *Jezebel*, a change-of-pace role as a woman (category: abandoned, but faithful wife) who lives through the San Francisco earthquake and remains loyal and

loving to her raffish husband. It was a performance in every way the reverse of Julie; and as audiences had lived through MGM's earthquake in *San Francisco* a mere two years before, it was even more of a tribute to her understated acting that she stopped film-goers' eyes straying to the Warner Bros rubble in the hope, perhaps, of seeing Gable, Tracy and Jeanette MacDonald among it.

As the 1930s neared an end, the nature of the 'woman's picture' was changing, as the position of women in American society evolved.

The country was climbing out of the Depression, though it would take the coming war effort to give the economy an extra heave back into boomtime. The 'bad news' for women was that this meant that the increasing number of new jobs were being filled by men. The economic liberation transiently achieved by women during the 1930s was not going to be repeated – or so it seemed until the outbreak of war – in the era of economic recovery. The

connection between this trend and the dimming of various stars' careers which took place simultaneously must always be speculative and tenuous: but the volume of Hollywood's output in those days, its speed, relative cheapness and permutations possible in star appeal, allowed the industry to react quickly, if not always rationally, to what it perceived to be a change in its audience's attitudes and preferences. The box-office was the only sure indicator: it was the reading of its entrails that produced the hit-or-miss mutations. The advertisement placed in a Hollywood trade paper by an independent exhibitors' association – i.e. those cinema owners not tied to any of the big studios – had said bluntly that some of the top-paid stars were box-office 'poison'. By itself, this judgement might be reversed by the next picture that one of those on the list was in: indeed all of them had hits within a year or two. But the advertisement's appearance confirmed the feeling in the always restless studio hierarchies that change was desirable.

JOAN BLONDELL

KAY FRANCIS

PATRICIA ELLIS

GLENDA FARRELL

MARION DAVIES

RUBY KEELER

MARGUERITE CHURCHILL

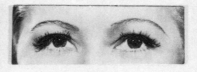

JOSEPHINE HUTCHINSON

BETTE DAVIS

MARGARET LINDSAY

ANITA LOUISE

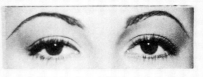

OLIVIA de HAVILLAND

WINIFRED SHAW

JEAN MUIR

JUNE TRAVIS

One change that came about was the humanizing of the screen's *femmes fatales*. In *Ninotchka*, Garbo was obliged to laugh; in *Destry Rides Again*, Dietrich got her bottom slapped by those boys in the back room. Stars already cast in the American image fared better: Ginger Rogers, Deanna Durbin, Jeanette MacDonald, Judy Garland became the favourites, as dancing dream-girls, singing sweethearts or visiting girls-next-door. Joan Crawford – even she! – had run out of re-creating herself every three or four years and was desperate enough to play an outright bitch in *The Women*, though, at Louis B. Mayer's insistence, she was allowed to go out on a catty joke that left her fur still sleek. The uppity society playgirl who had been humbled and democratized by a personable man of the people was on her way out, too: Katharine Hepburn's patrician brat in *The Philadelphia Story*, in 1940, seemed an eccentric hold-over. Having had Hollywood intervene on their behalf, reconciling the 'haves' to the 'have nots'

by using laughter or happy endings to iron out the social inequalities of the Depression era, the rich were gathering the reviving economy around them like protective coloration and were seldom to be seen again so prominently as characters in the movies. Bette Davis's next – and arguably most popular – part showed the evidence of this mutation.

It is odd, but one never thinks of Davis in *Dark Victory* (1939) as a rich socialite. But of course she is: what with her country mansion, servant, stable of racehorses, fur coats (including a fur cap that was to set a fashion trend for years) and the luxury of dying between chenille sheets.

It's not a sufficient answer to say that Judith Traherne – Davis's character – pays the price for enjoying unearned increment by expiring of a terminal disease. Nor even that there's a saving honesty in Davis's performance that pardons privilege. The answer lies in a quality she had never displayed on the screen – one that attracted the epithet of 'stoic', even 'beautiful'. That quality was *resignation*. Her old fighting phlegm is choked back in Casey Robinson's script and she surrenders to the only thing a Bette Davis character would have admitted was invincible – which is death itself.

Jack L. Warner hadn't favoured making the film: which immediately made her want to do it. In words that ironically anticipate the opening line of *Love Story*, one of the phenomenal best-sellers and hit movies of the 1970s, Warner remarked on the first day of shooting, 'I don't know who is going to want to see a picture about a girl who dies.'

He had bought the property – a play that David O. Selznick had once owned – in order to stop her nagging him; though Casey Robinson, one of the best craftsmen of 'woman's pictures' Hollywood produced, helped persuade him, too, arguing that work at Warners was making Davis 'too masculine' a property for her own or the studio's good. As he reworked it, the story lent her a fatefully resigned quality to redress the balance of her customary independence. In *Dark Victory*, she matches undertone to understatement. 'Confidentially, darling, this is more than a hangover,' she murmurs to her best friend (Geraldine Fitzgerald), turning her death sentence almost into an 'aside'. The invention of this 'best friend' – a character absent from the play – was a master-stroke and shows the care lavished at that era on every detail that could build up a film-star performance. For she is the chosen mouthpiece to relay all the anxieties, fears, bitterness that Davis didn't now need to let fall from her lips – lips that usually were smacked with relish at the thought of uttering such greedy emotions. Davis is allowed only one outburst of self-pity and professional reproach to her doctor (the long-serving George Brent) for concealing the truth about her incurable condition: for the remainder of the film, she bathes in a glow of remission which should almost get a separate photographic credit, growing more physically beautiful as the tumour works its worst. It is shameless dramaturgy: it is also stupendously effective.

Even one of Davis's trademarks, lighting up a cigarette, is turned to account. It's her *failure* to perform what's almost a Bette Davis rite with customary speed and efficiency that first hints at a serious dislocation of her motor faculties. 'Audience and doctor know,' notes the critic Charles Affron, 'that when Bette Davis can't light her own cigarette something is seriously amiss.'

In another way, too, Warner's top female star is transfigured by this film: it doesn't *feel* like a Warner film at all. It's been turned into the sort of movie closer to the heart of MGM: wholly sympathetic heroine, nobility of soul, strong but not disfiguring emphasis on suffering and, technically, a fondness for close-ups of prefiguring emotion when the camera settles on Davis's face and she seems to hold her thoughts 'still' for us to read the way that people being X-rayed are instructed to 'hold' their breath so as not to blur the plate. These are the trademarks of the polished MGM style.

97

With Bogart in *Dark Victory* (1939), the first of her great 'weepies'.

Opposite, her own marriage breaking up while making *Dark Victory*, she transferred her anxiety on to the character of a 'woman with everything' . . . who loses her most precious possession, her sight.

98

Mayer and Thalberg insisted that whatever their female stars did at MGM, they should do 'like ladies'. Davis lives like a lady – and dies like one. Part of the explanation for this is, of course, that she was directed by Edmund Goulding, who had first made her feel 'special' in that MGM way when he had directed her in *That Certain Woman* two years earlier. Goulding had fallen from grace at MGM because he had a drink problem and an independent mind: but he brought over from that studio and his work with stars like Crawford and Garbo a perception of women as 'special' beings. It was the antithesis of the way Jack L. Warner perceived them: but the rival studio may have even been in Warner's thoughts, as he had tried borrowing Spencer Tracey from Louis B. Mayer to play Davis's doctor and future husband. And surely it wasn't coincidence that as early as 1935, David O. Selznick had recommended *Dark Victory* to Garbo in the (vain) hope it would break her fondness for unprofitable historical pictures in

which she kept dates with death or destiny and lure her into 'a smart, modern picture' in which such things were to be had more cheaply on a domestic scale.

While *Dark Victory* was shooting, Davis's husband was preparing to divorce her. The action was heard soon after the picture was finished. It was an unusual case, even by Hollywood standards. The defects that other female stars usually attributed to their husbands in similar actions were this time imputed to his wife by the husband. She had been inattentive, casual and indifferent to him, he alleged; had become enraged and insulting. She ignored his friends; absented herself from meals; humiliated him in front of the household – and so on, for pages. It was 'role reversal' with a vengeance. The allegations of Hollywood divorces provided sad but striking testimony to the difficulty Davis had in reconciling the temperament that had contributed to the success of her work with a disposition that might have made for a happy marriage.

Some years later, interviewed by Rex Reed, she was characteristically forthright: 'If I had to do it all over again, the only thing I'd change is that I would never get married . . . My biggest problem all my life was men. I was a good wife. But I don't know any other lady in my category who (held on to) a husband either, unless she married for money or married a secretary-manager type where there was no competition. That's a price I've paid for success and I've had a lot of it.'

The uncontested action cost Davis dear: otherwise, it did not detract from her reputation by one jot. *Dark Victory* was not released until April 1939. Fans hadn't seen it when they read Harmon Nelson's harsh testimony: but they *had* seen Davis in *Jezebel* and knew she had won the 'Oscar' for the way she behaved in that film – and they simply saw the divorce-court testimony as confirmation of the way they would have expected 'Jezebel' to behave. In fact, had she presented herself as the aggrieved plaintiff, she might have suffered professional damage from the image confusion. But her forthright bitchiness actually protected her. It is worth adding that with other stars, other moral ironies applied. Joan Crawford, for instance, was mercifully spared the pain of posthumous exposure (by her adopted daughter) as a woman who had manufactured an image of public rectitude and maternal love, whereas she was alleged to have been a monster of duplicity – and worse. Yet this revelation coincided with the cynicism of a 1970s' generation which couldn't believe that any star, in life or on the screen, could have been such a paragon, anyhow. When Faye Dunaway played Joan Crawford in the movie *Mommie Dearest* and attacked her screen daughter with the famous cheap wire coathanger, at least one California audience chanted approvingly, 'Kill, Joan, kill. . . .' They, too, expected even a surrogate Crawford to live up to her screen image.

Davis's divorce left its pain; but her Oscar for *Jezebel* and the adulatory reviews of *Dark*

Victory removed the sting. (Frank E. Nugent, in *The New York Times*, said she should have received the Academy Award for the *latter* picture.) She even had the sweet bonus of praise for her relatively small part in *Juarez* (1939), which had been premiered *one week* after *Dark Victory*. In this Paul Muni vehicle, undertaken by Warner Bros to help the State Department counter the influence of the Axis and Fascist powers in Latin America, she played the Empress Carlotta of Mexico. Erupting into the presence of the Emperor Louis Napoleon (Claude Rains) in a fury over his betrayal of her puppet husband, she fills the ample space of the palace drawing-room like a storm cloud, buffeting about the room, then, more alarmingly, all passion discharged, lapsing into a motionless black coma on the *chaise longue*. Many another actress exhausted by the strain of dying beautifully in *Dark Victory* might have passed up the chance to go out of her mind in *Juarez*. But not Davis. Maybe it was a relief to be able to lose her temper again.

Below, as the Empress Carlotta (with Emperor Brian Aherne) in *Juarez* (1939): a historical vehicle virtually immobilised by its own stateliness.

From this time on, many of Davis's roles focus on anxieties familiar enough to all women and made especially poignant by the actress personifying them: motherhood and the wilfulness of children, ageing and the loss of looks, spinsterhood, loss of social status and financial insecurity. Issues that were the inevitable lot of woman passing through the middle age of their emotions now stretched Davis to far greater advantage than those of possessing or destroying a man had done in earlier films. Strong-willed stars sometimes use roles to invent experience that they themselves can't enjoy off screen – or, at least, haven't up to then.

For a star with an unrivalled talent for the understanding of women, Davis had until then been living a peculiarly restricted, unrewarding life off screen. And with the break-up of her marriage, and her ex-husband's immediate flight as far away from California as possible, there was even less for her to come home to. Considering this relative famine of emotional nourishment, the feast of womanly experience she now proceeded to serve up in her film roles is truly astonishing. But there were other reasons for it, too.

The cinema audience changed dramatically with America's entry into the European war: it became predominantly female. This was true of the labour front, too. Since the majority of able-bodied males not in reserved occupations were drafted into the forces, women replaced them in office and factory until, by 1943, they were estimated at nearly forty per cent of the workforce. Hollywood's male stars were liable to the draft, too; and the actresses temporarily abandoned by the likes of Clark Gable, James Stewart, Melvyn Douglas and the rest had to make do with co-stars who were either younger or older than themselves or else not in the same bracket of stardom. Either way, the accent of interest was placed on females; their relations with men were, more often than not, observed from their viewpoint. Women stars enjoyed a tremendous and unexpected new prominence.

101

And women audiences, suffering from the lack of men about the house but rapidly finding compensation in doing a man's job at the office desk or assembly line, looked to the screen to reflect their emancipation – and not only in movies about female riveters, front-line nurses and soldier girls. They wanted movies to offer them consolation or catharsis for the ways that women coped with . . . well, with being women. Bette Davis supplied much of this succour and solidarity.

The films she made in the last few months of peace left her well placed to ride the powerful surge of her sex's ambitions which the war released. *The Old Maid* (1939) was her first venture into frustrated motherhood. A period piece directed by Edmund Goulding, it is about a woman who starts a home for orphans from the American Civil War in order to find a respectable hiding place for her own illegitimate child by the officer who had been her lover before being killed in battle. She later has to watch the little girl being reared by her selfish cousin (played by Davis's old rival Miriam Hopkins) who is regarded by the infant as her

Perc Westmore applies the make-up: fading beauty
attracted someone never gratified by her own looks from
the start.

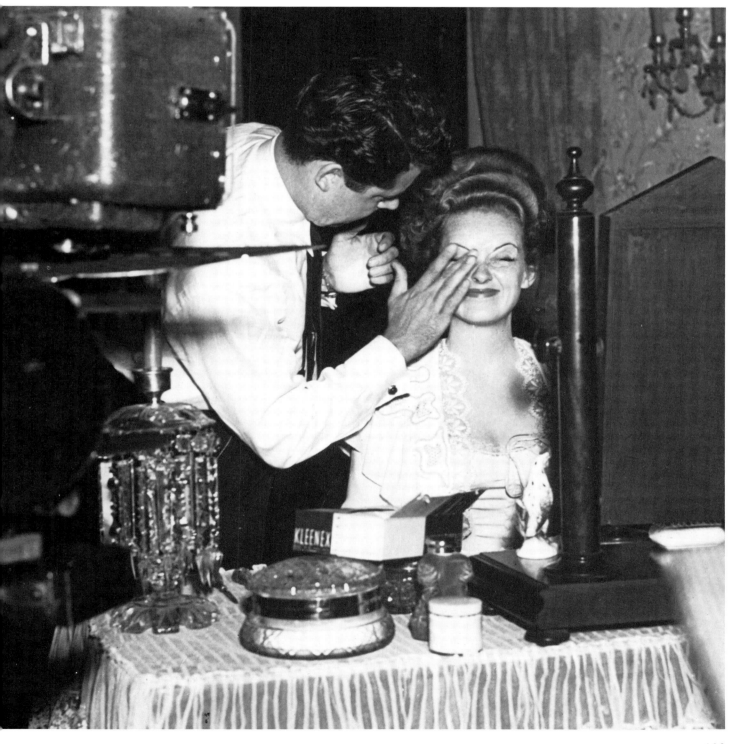

honorary mama – while looking, in ignorance and pity, on her real mother as simply an 'old maid' aunt. It sounds both schematic and schmaltzy. That is not how it plays. Davis preserves the woman's integrity by the unusual composure of her face, storing emotions at a far deeper level than before, and making her co-star seem to overwork at the business of being maternally ingratiating. This was the strategy she employed every time Hopkins was cast with (or against) her in a film. Davis lets *the movie* work for her as she watches the shadows of Hopkins and the little girl pass up the staircase wall, the woman's arm round the child's shoulder, become magnified by the illumination and they pass from sight, taking with them all Bette's hopes and love. Goulding keyed her scenes so that her moral self-reproach never turns into self-indulgent masochism. Graham Greene wrote: 'Great actresses choose odd mediums and perhaps Miss Davis is a great actress. Her performance ... is of extraordinary virtuosity – as the young girl, as the secret mother and as the harsh, prim middle-aged woman.'

Perc Westmore, her make-up man, trusted her acting powers so completely that he eschewed the usual way of denoting age by pencilling in lines on an actress's face: all he used was a pale, liquid wash which 'faded' her as it dried. She did the rest by herself: she was 'old' in thought.

The ageing process fascinated Davis, especially as it affected lonely women. It allowed her to feed into her star persona one of the commonest apprehensions known to women. And anyhow, fading beauty was a very satisfying card for someone to play who never flattered herself on her own looks in the first place. Thus it was with relish that she went into the role of Queen Elizabeth I – a woman more than twice her age.

Watchful, proud, devious, distrustful, ruthless: her Tudor monarch maintains her absolutism in ways that had obvious affinities with Davis's own experience of how treacherous human relationships could be. For queen and star, work was a surer satisfaction. Statecraft relates to stardom, too. The palace protocol in Maxwell Anderson's verse play on which *The Private Lives of Elizabeth and Essex* was based parallels the pecking order of a film studio in ways too obvious to need more than a mention. In this film, and in *The Virgin Queen* (1955), the darker, sourer one she later made about the same Elizabeth, she gave full rein to what was now a fixed and feared characteristic of hers – sarcasm. She had developed a talent for public rebuke that added a curare tip to an already sharp tongue. Ultimately, it was a talent she took to mimicking – though seldom wholly deriding – since she knew by then the relish that audiences got from even the mock displeasure she vented on the right occasion. In later years, when addressing large, gleefully anticipatory assemblies of fans who had been fed excerpts from her films and were still hungry for the lady herself, she would come on stage, shoot a disdainful look out front and exclaim, 'What a dump!' The same sarcastic temperament was what the two Tudor dramas 'institutionalized' in the personage of a queen who is officially 'unanswerable'. When in the film Errol Flynn does answer her back, she exercises another royal prerogative – and boxes his ears. Fear that Davis might do the same to 'nosy' interviewers later made many of them keep a prudent distance from her.

The casting of Flynn displeased her. She had been yearning for Laurence Olivier, whose *Wuthering Heights* (directed by Davis's old love William Wyler) had its American première just as the 'royal' film started shooting in April 1939. Three years earlier, speaking to an English journalist, she had said, 'Perhaps in Britain, where individuality is more strongly developed, it is performance rather than personality which counts. I should very much like to find out for myself, and I intend to make a film in England the very first chance I get.' How welcome the experience of co-starring with Davis would have been to Olivier is a mat-

104

The magnificence of majesty: unfortunately it left little free with which to act – hence her more than usual reliance on her voice to animate a State portrait.

The luxury of ageing: playing Queen Elizabeth allowed her to wallow in make-up (including a balding cranium) that exposed the vulnerability of the queen as a woman.

And, seeking relief from affairs of State with Olivia de Havilland.

ter of speculation. He has since admitted to emerging from Wyler's direction as if from an acid bath – all the snobbish condescension he had brought with him into films from the stage having been eaten off him by that dedicated film-maker's corrosive tongue. But there can be little doubt that he would have made an invigorating counter-weight to Davis. Though just a year older than she was, he was ripe for the youthful glow of dangerous conceit that gave the Earl of Essex his aura of fascination for the Queen: Olivier's very 'Englishness' served the same function for Davis. She had desperately wanted to play Cathy opposite his Heathcliff in *Wuthering Heights*. Having now to accept Flynn was a double disappointment. She may have looked for compensation in the extraordinary elaborate attention she paid to her own looks as Elizabeth: denied her own 'favourite', she made sure it would be a one-woman show.

Her round featured face was logically quite wrong for the penduncular looks of the sixty-five-year-old Elizabeth. But she both wrought and *willed* herself into an uncanny likeness of her, gaining the effect of a living effigy by thinning her mouth to a Tudor lip-line, shaving her eyebrows completely off and then having a single line painted in, much as a contemporary Tudor miniaturist might have been obliged to represent majesty by a stroke. Not only did she give a balding effect to her frontal cranium by shaving part of her pate, but she extended the look of bare effrontery to her already prominent eyeballs by having her eye-lashes camouflaged by flesh-coloured wax.

Bearing in mind Elizabeth's belligerent declaration to her troops at Tilbury that she had 'the Body of a weak and female Woman but . . . the Heart and Stomach of a King,' she lowered the register of her voice several tones so as to intensify the impression of a male spirit in a female container.

Colour photography, being used in a Davis film for the first time and at precisely the right moment in her career, enhanced the illusion she gave of a State portrait – but an *animate* one.

107

Ex-king meets reigning queen: Charles Laughton, who had played Henry VIII six years earlier, visits the set to pay his respects to his Tudor descendant. 'Never stop daring to hang yourself, Bette,' he advised, somewhat inappositely. The Tudors risked losing all at a stroke.

Deprived by her wide crinoline and bejewelled upper structure of much chance to express emotions by her body, she relied more than usually on voice, hands and features. As so many of her speeches had to begin at top pitch and work up to a dramatic climax, it is no surprise that she burst several blood vessels in her throat and had to endure a few days' enforced silence.

Male and female characteristics seem to be using the Queen's person as a battleground. But as in her performance just prior to this picture, what humanizes this Elizabeth is the emergence of the 'old maid' in her nature. For just before she sets eyes for the last time on the Earl of Essex, imprisoned in the Tower of London, the Queen primps and titivates herself for an instant like millions of ordinary women in every age and place putting on their best face for a lover – even though this one, by her command, is due to lose his head. It cannot be said that Elizabeth loses her youth: but in that flurry of concern for her looks, Davis drives home the vulnerability to which age exposes king, queen or commoner.

Off the set, she spoke a bit like the opinionated monarch she played. The tenor and content of her interviews resembled prose *précis* of Maxwell Anderson's versified thesis about the loneliness of absolute power when the person possessing it wants to temper it with love, but cannot make her own will bend to accept love when a man offers it to her, lest it is construed as weakness. In the light of her broken marriage, her opinions assume a therapeutic force. Not exactly a 'true confession': but true enough to what marriage had taught her about men – and herself. 'Men continually work and fret themselves into bad tempers over their sex's resentment of women's new-found independence in their careers,' she told a *Photoplay* interviewer. '[But] women never have, never will be, never can be independent of the men they love – and be happy! All women know this. Only men are blind to it. . . . Men should boss women more. This is particu-

larly true of American men. Women adore feeling they are possessed, that they belong to a dominant male. . . . All men need to do is quit pouting over their lack of dominance and begin to assert it more. The women won't mind. They'll love it!' There spoke the woman. In her memoirs, twenty-three years later, it emerged that she divided *man*kind into 'men' and 'male stars', and of the latter she was to speak less benignly: 'There wasn't a fistful I could even have a conversation with, and with the solitary exception of the powerhouse (Wyler?) who would have threatened my career, not one I could look up to in respect. They were on the whole a lot of weak sisters who were attracted to sovereignty and were frightened by it.' There spoke the queen.

Making *Elizabeth and Essex* took its toll on her health. She had been averaging three films a year. And her insistence on her right to be consulted, to warn and to advise – the prerogatives of English monarchs – made for a greater strain than when she had been 'simply' a bid-

den actress. She retreated to New England and there, like a female Anteus, tried to draw up new vigour from her native earth. Having lost a husband, she now gained a home, buying and refurbishing an old New Hampshire mansion which she named 'Butternut'. At the same time, almost in the same place, she found in Arthur Farnsworth the man who was to become her new husband. The son of a land-owning family which had fallen on lean times, he was like her house, of venerable Yankee stock. They met at a local inn where he was working as a clerk-receptionist and felt an immediate sympathy of background. They got married barely a year later, on New Year's Eve, 1940, when Farnsworth was out on the coast paying Bette a visit. As if seeking to isolate herself even further from the encircling film world, she had acquired a new home there, too, a house named 'Riverbottom' in Glendale, near Griffith Park, which she furnished like a New England cottage. It is curious how many of the stars who came to movies from theatrical careers in the East demonstrated their alienation from – or, at best, their independence of – the 'Dream Factory' that gave them fame and wealth by adopting a predominantly New England style of life, even extending it to the architecture of their homes. (Nowadays, of course, they would simply go on living in the East and commute to Hollywood.) Henry Fonda, Davis's one-time college date, who came from New York Dutch stock, had bought a twenty-four-acre farm built of artificially weathered wood in suburban Brentwood whose dinner bell could be heard by the folks in Beverly Hills whenever it was rung in the roof-turret. Even the inescapable Hollywood obligation to have a swimming pool had been partially circumvented by disguising it to look like a country duck-pond. This style soon became a realtor's cliché. But for Bette Davis and like-minded 'settlers', it remained a moral bastion: to the Hollywood people, it said, 'Keep Your Distance'.

Her first film after a five-month recuperation protracted by studio wrangles over pay and

All This and Heaven Too (1940), a sombre period piece,
allowed her to demonstrate her skill at revealing what was
in her mind without much physical effort.

Below in *The Letter* (1940) she played virtually the whole
part from the opening moment when she shoots her lover
to the last scene when she meets her own fate in the moonlit
garden without exposing the deceit that her looks
concealed and, opposite, her ruthless composure is total.

scripts was a sombre period piece, *All This and
Heaven Too* (1940), directed by Anatol Litvak.
Based on a famous murder which happened in
Paris in 1843, it cast her as a French governess
in a ducal family. Charles Boyer was the Duke.
Davis would have preferred to be his duchess
(and murder victim); but she used the part as
a chance to see how much emotion she could
project with the least physical effort. Her face
is unusually composed: yet her thoughts never
find a hiding place on it – they are always being
forced into the open.

It was a good practice piece for her next film
and the one that many consider the finest she
ever made: the role of a woman who, conversely, spends the whole picture concealing
her thoughts, lying to cover them up.

The Letter (1940) re-united her with William
Wyler through another 'loan-out' arrange-
ment. Wyler, who was under contract to Goldwyn, was lent to Warner Bros in return for
Warner's lending Davis to Goldwyn for the
film he was preparing of *The Little Foxes*.
Clearly her career had reached its peak in
power and prestige. Now her performance followed suit.

The Letter isn't about a woman in love: it
is about a liar in a trap. Leslie Crosby, the
adulterous wife who fires six shots into her
faithless lover in the gripping opening, perjures
herself in court, then persuades her lawyer into
collusion with her and deceives the jury in
order to escape the hangman. Deceit becomes
Davis marvellously: it sharpens her femininity.
She never seems more desirable than when she
is lying her way out of a crisis with a ready
tongue and, if that fails, falling back on wiles
and pleas that are pitched at the male she basically mistrusts and despises. A similar dilemma
was to form the basis of *In This Our Life* (1942),
directed by John Huston, which produced the
same seductive dissimulation in her spoilt
Southern girl (also extending her ambiguity
into her name: this time 'Stanley Timberlake')
who gets involved in a hit-and-run accident
and tries to lie her way out of it. Both films

110

were set in communities – Asian in one case, Southern black in the other – where the whites are a privileged minority, and Davis's flagrant disregard of guilt has racial undertones that give her performance a particularly decadent resonance. She will save her own skin at the price of people whose skin already places them in an inferior relationship. The 'superior' race of British colonials in *The Letter* is the arrogant coloration that Davis adds to a character who otherwise hides her true complexion.

Her performance gains in intensity from the mastery she now brings to the virtues of stillness. Her acting is all of a piece now and a true *cinema* experience. Jezebel and all her bitchy sorority sisters from earlier films are show-offs compared with Leslie Crosbie, whose patient crocheting of the lace mantilla that grows with her lies like a web of deceit, until it becomes a winding-sheet in wait for the stroke of retribution delivered off screen in the last minutes, reflects the actress's own seamless concentration. In the final resort, when cornered in a lie, she can always faint – but even then, in total stillness, she seems to show a mind still working to deceive. Even the jury's acquittal produces no private repentance. Just the contrary. Remaining obsessively attached to the man she murdered, she tells her husband that that's the way it is to be; and her unflinching posture presages the monumental immobility she assumes in Wyler's later film, *The Little Foxes*, when the same actor, Herbert Marshall, in the same husbandly role, suffers his cardiac attack in her unmoved (and unmoving) presence.

By suppressing Davis's emotions, Wyler exposed her genius. He used quite lengthy camera takes in *The Letter* and the cast were forced to pick their physical steps and verbal phrasing through a complicated maze of 'marks' on the set arranged for the photographer Tony Gaudio. In *The Little Foxes*, with Gregg Toland behind the camera, the visual 'depth of focus' that Toland gave Wyler's direction served the same purpose,

communication of emotion, sometimes at a considerable distance from the lens, but always intimately. Charles Affron has noted how Davis's 'enormous eyes [in *The Letter*] are integrated into the film's visual and dramatic designs, its opening and closing blinds.' The moon's eye, too, turns coldly on her (unseen) murder in the garden at the end. Even her dead lover's Chinese mistress (played, though, by the Caucasian actress Gale Sondergaard in Oriental make-up) has the snake-eyes that in the version of *The Letter* made by Jean de Limur in 1928, starring Jeanne Eagles in the Davis role, were replicated by the actual reptile in the fight between a mongoose and a cobra in the brothel where Leslie Crombie went to buy back the incriminating letter. With Davis on hand this time, there is no need for the director to turn the menagerie loose.

The extraordinary stillness of her performance can best be judged by the sole movement of alarm that she makes – the only one that shows her vulnerability. The Asian woman looks disdainfully down at her in one of Wyler's favourite sharp angles of jeopardy and forces the white woman to stoop and retrieve the all-important letter she has deliberately let fall at her feet. As Davis does so, the other woman steps back – as if making ready to strike her head off. Davis freezes. The reflex is clearly based on a movement of the animal kingdom: self-abasement in order to deflect danger. A second later, she is herself again.

If it is the woman's privilege to change her mind – a comment on inconstancy that sounds like the invention of a male chauvinist – then Davis's achievement in *The Letter* is to show a woman who does *not* change her mind. She is without a nerve in her body: her composure is total: the very spectacles she puts on at times of crisis to do her lace work add another cold-paned screen between her true nature and us.

If *The Letter* exemplified perverse psychology at its most heartless, Davis's other film with Wyler, *The Little Foxes* (1941), illustrates relentless cupidity. This is what makes

112

it somewhat the lesser film. In it Regina Giddens is basically a mercenary woman; and the exercise of power to such an ignoble end robs the character of the interior flux of emotions contained in *The Letter*. Wyler wanted Davis to soften Regina's single-mindedness, but to no avail. She went after the woman's managerial malevolence which freezes her to the spot where she is sitting, back turned to her stricken husband as he crawls up the stairs like a man on a cliff face to get to the heart drops that may save his life – but cost Regina her business fortune. The camera holds on her, not looking but listening, concentrating on her mental image of the stricken man as clearly as if the scene were being reflected back to her at the acute angle of her gaze in a mirror that is just out of camera range.

Her husband's death puts Regina's larcenous brother in her power and makes her a partner in the sweatshop cotton mill. Since concupiscence is her driving force this time, not deceit, Davis narrowed her eyes by extended false lashes and the thin wash of calomine lotion she put on her face gave her a constipated look to match the over-stuffed furnish-

ings of the period. Her hair-style, rolled into a high Edwardian pompadour, recalls Disney's Evil Queen in *Snow White*, which had been released three years earlier. She seems to be constantly using an accountant's ruler to draw a merciless bottom line under her cold profession of avarice; 'I don't ask for things I don't think I can get.'

Within months of the film's completion, America had entered the war; and women were flowing into the jobs vacated by men. It was like the breaking up of a gender log-jam. Having been dependent on husbands earning a living, women now discovered what it was like to have an income of their own and be managing the family finances. 'Money', if not earned income, had already been part and parcel of the American woman's life, enshrined in the divorce and testamentary laws of the country, never mind the double indemnity clauses of insurance policies on husbands with shorter life spans than their wives. In short, money was an economic fact of life for American woman to a far greater degree than in most other countries; the war economy simply delivered 'the goods' more directly and perhaps earlier. A woman who went after money the way Regina did evoked an understanding, if not sympathy. Davis even recalled hearing of a lady who turned to her female companion after they had both seen *The Little Foxes* and said, 'True to life, isn't it?' Probably it was even truer to fantasy: killing one's husband, by calculation or neglect, was a fantasy with some appeal in an economy where women's rights were recognized sooner than they were in other sectors of life. It was money that purchased Leslie Crombies's acquittal in *The Letter*, only it was her husband who had to shell it out. In *The Little Foxes*, Herbert Marshall pays an even stiffer price – his life. But this time Regina remains alive to be a free woman and profit from her inheritance. Despite a final shot of her daughter deserting her to join the beau who has been waiting in the rain, signifying that Regina has only the loneliness of old age to anticipate,

this simply looked like a gestural bit of morality tacked on to the film as the price exacted by the Hays Office for not insisting on her meeting with physical retribution. The fact that Lillian Hellman's play had been a huge and *recent* Broadway success protected the film-makers against the Hollywood censor's insistence on 'compensating moral values' better than if it had been an as yet undramatized best-selling novel. But Davis's creation of mercenary heartlessness is such that few film-goers could have imagined Regina would grieve over-much, or for long. Like Scarlett O'Hara, another lady abandoned at the end of a film, she would probably postpone crying until tomorrow, at least.

Although sibling jealousy, not money, was the theme of *In This Our Life*, two pictures later, her Stanley Timberlake is as morally stone-deaf as Regina Giddens: no use using the voice of conscience against her eardrum. Davis played a modern miss who steals her sister's man, marries him, dumps him, allies herself with another woman who is a caricature of the man-eating American wife and finally runs over a mother and child in her convertible and tries to pin the blame on a black boy: such wilfulness adds up to more lines on the moral charge sheet than Regina's old-fashioned embrace of only one of the deadly sins. But Stanley's creed also comes from wealth, from her rich uncle (Charles Coburn) who keeps her supplied with the pocket money that is Hollywood's way of hinting indirectly at incestuous affection. Her creed is spelled out as directly as Regina's: 'What we want we go after and what we go after we get.' This avaricious echo in the dialogue is no accident: the screen writer of both films was Howard Koch. At this fruitful stage in her choice of roles, one can trace the genes being transmitted from one to the next.

In This Our Life, however, was an unexpected flop. Davis candidly attributed it to looking too old for the part: she was thirty-three at the time. Whatever the cause, she didn't accept

another 'pure evil' role in a hurry; and when next she did, in *A Stolen Life* (1946), she hedged her bets by playing identical twins, one bad, one good. In fact she had grown adept at switching from sympathetic roles to their opposite and back again. It stretched her, she said: and for once, it was in line with Warner Bros production policy. 'Davis – Sweet or Sour' was the recipe. Guessing which she would be next appealed to audiences.

Having a child, or indeed *not* having a child but adopting someone else's, was a strategy successfully used several times to focus the attention of the women. *The Great Lie* (1941) offered the added attraction – or so some chauvinist male critics of the day saw it – of dealing in the sort of fibs 'neither great nor especially blameworthy.' as Bosley Crowther characterized them, which are held to appeal to women in particular. In this case, it is Davis's lie to George Brent on his returning home unexpectedly after he had been given up for lost on an aircraft flight that the baby she

presents to him is their own. It is, in fact, his offspring by Davis's rival (Mary Astor), an international concert pianist who had learnt too late that her marriage to Brent was invalid. The two women represent a nicely balanced view of their sex's virtues and vices. Bette is the natural home-maker (provided Hattie McDaniel and other lovable black retainers are there to do the donkey work on her estate). An outdoor girl of the shirt and pants variety, she effortlessly wins the women's vote by kicking off her shoes to curl up on the sofa. Mary is the over-strung woman of artistic sensibility – otherwise known to Hollywood as a bitch – who slaps her *masseuse*'s face for being too rough and is snappish to long-distance operators struggling to put through calls. The film's trick is to let *her* (who doesn't want it) have the baby and Bette (who does want it, but hasn't had it) adopt the infant. Will she, won't she be allowed to keep it – never mind her secret? Again the director was Edmund Goulding, who treated it all as a light-weight tease.

Opposite, a modern miss again, but still greedy: as Stanley Timberlake who steals her sister's man in *In This Our Life* (1942). Below, 'Here Astor, let's go talk a minute.' Bette and Mary Astor put their heads together to improve a soap-opera plot in *The Great Lie* (1941) into something in which women could recognise themselves. Though Astor played an international concert pianist and Davis a well-off gal with no ties, they brought to the dilemma of the unmarried mother a plausible reality. And right, Perc Westmore and photographer Tony Gaudio lent the film their kind of 'reality' as well.

But one surprising feature in this repressive era of Hollywood censorship is to find the two women, who have become tolerant friends in their hour of mutual need, putting in time together in an up-country shack while one of them has an illegitimate baby. It is quite a lengthy sequence in the film; and for two women to share the screen together without men for that span of time was then a rarity in films – always, of course, excepting *The Women*, whose men are expressly written out of the story.

In one of her volumes of memoirs, Mary Astor lays a lot of the success for this (like the baby itself) at Davis's doorstep. 'One morning Bette said to me in a very peremptory manner, "Hey, Astor, let's go talk a minute."' This was usually a sinister sign; and Astor had already noted the way Davis's hitherto overly benign attitude to her before filming began had changed into a brusqueness during the shooting, when she would sit on the set, critically watching the players and swinging her foot

ominously like a cat's tail. 'I had the old "what have I done now?" feeling [but] she flopped on the couch and said, "This picture is going to stink. It's too incredible for words . . . I can't get anywhere up front unless I have something to offer that will make it better. You've got to help." How? "You and I, really just us. . . . All I do is mewl to George [Brent] about 'that woman you married when you were drunk' and to 'please come back to me' and all that crap. And that's just soap opera."' Davis then proposed that she and Astor put their heads together before the day's work, and indeed during the day's shooting, and devise a relationship between the two women that wasn't 'soap opera'. They succeeded.

For a start, their bitchiness is played on the white notes – the original script, one is given to understand, had the loud pedal from the start. They even improved the story into plausible reality – that quality essential to Davis in order to feel it, show it and transcend it – when pregnancy forces a companionable truce on the

117

characters. Without losing her own feminine sympathy, Davis plays the paternal role, bawling out Astor for breaking her diet, contemptuously dismissing the prescribed 'ounce' of brandy ('Who ever heard of an "ounce" of brandy?') and pouring the mother-to-be a good manly dose and even slapping her when she gets hysterical to bring her to her matronly senses.

For her performance Mary Astor won the Oscar for Best Supporting Actress. At the ceremony, she thanked Tchaikovsky – and might have added Rabinowicz who had doubled for her on the concert grand. Then, to tremendous applause, she thanked Davis.

The Great Lie is something more than a film about small fibs. Davis had improved it into something more than plausibility. It is one of the few films reflecting the choices then facing unwed mothers, not to mention women who weren't mothers but wanted to be. Of course it's fortunate that surrogate motherhood is represented by as desirable a being as Bette Davis.

Davis hankered after comedy at this time: but she was by no means grateful to find herself cast opposite Cagney in *The Bride Came C.O.D.* (1941). *High* comedy was what she wanted; and being bent over Cagney's knee while he picked cactus prickles out of her backside was comedy in a rather lower bracket than pleased her. To go straight from this film to *The Little Foxes* certainly set the pendulum of public taste swinging wildly: but then she came out of *The Little Foxes* into another comedy, *The Man Who Came To Dinner* (1941), and this time fared better.

If Davis had not much to do in this vehicle for the Broadway actor Monty Woolly, who played the eponymous boor, she was probably glad to rest while others did the rushing around. Behind every great man stands a little woman: that just about sums up her role as sympathetic but firm secretary to the unbearable celebrity. But she shrewdly gauged how even this secondary position could be turned

to advantage in a 'change of pace' role: her moderation and common sense triumph over the madness of everyone else in her misanthropist employer's entourage. Remove the celebrity decoration and the name-dropping from the play – which Davis had actually asked Warners to buy for her, hoping she would get to play opposite John Barrymore whose theatrical legend she still respected, however destitute he and it had become – and what one is left with is another 'secretary versus wife' situation comedy. The twist, though, is that Davis doesn't want to marry her employer, but escape from him by becoming the wife of a nice young newsman. Women enjoyed the rebukes this self-possessed but 'ordinary' woman dealt out to her boss: many in the audience must have wished they could do the same in their own offices. At the same time, it was reassuring that she wanted to marry a non-celebrity. For the huge majority of Davis fans, this was 'just like life', too. Happiness with a nobody had to be most women's lot, if they were lucky. Whatever her private doubts, based on experience, Davis underwrote the choice in her role-playing.

We have her own assurance that the next 'sympathetic' movie she made brought her the most mail she had ever received from women – especially from the daughters of possessive mothers or from possessive mothers who had seen her performance as Charlotte Vale in *Now, Voyager* (1942) and had repented of their possessiveness.

That the film should have this cathartic effect is appropriate; for it was one of the first to exploit the popular appeal of psychiatry which the war and the battle-shocked servicemen in need of therapy were soon going to turn from a self-indulgent frill of affluent living into one of the necessities of American life. It dramatized an issue that Davis's correspondence revealed to be common in wartime American families where the father was away fighting – namely the effort of children to win independence from the maternal

Below, thanks to Davis's advice, Henreid was turned from gigolo-type into Euro-American charmer for *Now, Voyager*. Twenty-two years later, now her director on *Dead Ringer* (1964), Henreid re-creates the 'two cigarette' trick used in *Now, Voyager* to denote sexual passion: its possibilities for cancer were also limitless. Soap-opera iconography: women believed 'the man in the white tuxedo' could materialise for them, too, as he had for Bette, preferably by the rail of a luxury liner.

head of the house. It dramatized it, of course, in terms of sentimental drama – Davis's own liberation from a repressive matriarch (Gladys Cooper) her treatment by an all-wise analyst (Claude Rains) and her final cure by a charming man of the world (Paul Henreid), whose love for her will never have to stand the test of marriage since he already has a wife and family. Hence the last line, whose eminently mimicable quality has made it one of the most famous in movie dialogue: 'Oh, Jerry, we have the stars, let's not ask for the moon.'

It was a very clever script – Casey Robinson again – playing on womanly fears but offering ultimate reassurance – in short, promising film-goers the stars (if not the moon).

The plot appealed to a side of Davis that was to become more evident with age and the power to pick her roles – the 'changeling' device that allows her to enjoy two quite different kinds of character inside the same film by transforming one into the other. Charlotte Vale (Davis) is an ugly duckling at the start of the film. Her pudding-plainness is exposed in segments as she descends the staircase (scene of so many Bette Davis epiphanies) and enters her

mother's palatial but cold drawing-room with the hostile rain so beloved by director Irving Rapper beating on the window panes to meet the Merlin-figure of Rains's analyst. First come the un-chic shoes, then a shapeless body, finally a bespectacled face hard with suspicion – and harder still from what looks like quick-setting concrete applied as face powder. A few months later, the same graduated revelation announces the miracle that has taken place thanks to psychiatry – two-toned high-fashion shoes, trim form, tweezed eyebrows and the familiar Bette Davis mouth. Her homecoming, even more confident of the inner woman after meeting Henreid on the ocean cruise, completes the evolutionary cycle. 'Yes, William, it's me,' she quips sardonically to the Nob Hill butler – and prepares the way of 'me' to become 'us' as Henreid turns up at one of the receptions she starts throwing for the Boston Social Register.

Henreid was ten years older than Boyer; but, like him, he used his European accent to seductive effect, simulating a tenderness and patience in love that possibly gratified American women more than their countrymen's brusque ideas of courtship. In *Now, Voyager*, he makes his char-

acter into every woman's dream lover. Davis at first had resisted his casting after seeing a make-up test that turned him into a gigolo type. She asked Hal Wallis to let him make a new test and this time approved the blend of Euro-American charmer.

All Hollywood films of this period had to find ways of suggesting the mutual attraction leading up to presumed sexual intercourse without being explicit; and *Now, Voyager* devised a way that has entered into screen iconography, it became so widely imitated and at the same time affectionately mocked. This is the trick with the two cigarettes which Henreid put between his lips, lighted both, then handed one of them to the expectant Davis. In the Olive Higgins Prouty novel published the year before, such emblematic intercourse was achieved slightly differently. The woman lit the man's cigarette: he handed it to her in return for the match: then he lit his own. But a burning match is even more temperamental than the enflamed passion it connotes. So at some point in the scripting or, more likely, the rehearsal, someone (and there are several claimants) suggested reverting to the scene in *The Rich Are Always with Us*, ten years earlier, in which George Brent also lit cigarettes for two. Davis had been a supporting player in that film – and later confessed she had conceived an unrequited attraction to Brent who was to make eleven films with her. The cigarette 'gimmick' worked for the 'consenting parties' of *Now, Voyager* so memorably that this film is often credited with conceiving it. What its popularity did for lung-cancer statistics in the years ahead is unthinkable.

Since Henreid played one of those unhappily married men who are too noble to make their wives suffer by getting up and leaving them – a breed known mainly to Hollywood writers with lay and religious censors to consider – Davis had to remain a childless mistress with only, one presumes, the occasional 'cigarette' to draw on. But that only reinforced the wish-fulfilment feature of a film that later generations look on with the indulgence granted High Kitsch. The absolute confidence that Hollywood had in its audience's taste and how it could be manipulated – it must be said with consummate shrewdness and skill – is seldom better exemplified in any other 1940s film. It has remained one of Davis's few favourites.

Jack L. Warner expressed his gratitude practically – he raised her salary to $2,500 a week.

But an even greater orgy of self-sacrifice awaited her in *Old Acquaintance* (1943), John Van Druten's play about a twenty-year love-hate relationship between old friends who are the best of enemies. Miriam Hopkins was cast as the bitch after various actresses had refused to play such so 'unsympathetic' a role; and Davis was the 'best friend', although she said she'd be happy in either part. *Old Acquaintance* marks the high tide-mark of the 'woman's picture' of the 1940s. In it is just about every self-consciously 'big' scene that the genre could ask for. Among them: Bette finding that Miriam's husband is in love with her; Bette herself falling for a young lover half her age; Bette discovering Miriam's daughter is in love with this boy; Bette laying hands on Hopkins and literally shaking common sense into her; Hopkins's daughter being re-introduced to her estranged father by Bette; Bette rescuing the girl from a Park Avenue wolf; women being bitchy to each other in luxury; women being loyal to their country in wartime; Hopkins's tireless self-dramatizing; Bette's unselfish generosity. . . . Such a scenario, the work of various hands including Edmund Goulding and Howard Koch, though credited to Van Druten and Leonore Coffee, put female film-goers over every hurdle on the emotional sprinting track. It is played for all it is worth – and more. Rematching old rivals like Davis and Hopkins produces a chemical reaction even before a scene gets properly going. Yet it is far more than a two-handed version of *The Women* (with men present). It states, albeit in popular form, some very sympathetic truths about the sex in general.

It demonstrates, for example, that marriage and children are not the only things in life that a woman can aim for; nor does one have to turn into a neurotic old maid if one misses out on them. Davis remains unmarried in the film; and although this is a token of literary dedication rather than maternal disappointment, sublimating sexuality into productivity, she stays a warm-hearted, better balanced individual than the shrewish, selfish Hopkins who has both husband and family. A sentimental romantic in attitude, Hopkins's character is actually a sharp-clawed materialist. Davis begins the film as a convincing girl in her early twenties: the fact that she is a bit mannish round the edges in her tailored jacket, schoolboy shirt and tie and pocket hanky is merely Hollywood shorthand for how serious she is about the sort of writing that will be greeted by high praise and low sales. In everything to do with getting a man, she is on the losing side. Either she is too noble and won't steal Miriam's husband ('There are things you just don't do if you want to live with yourself decently afterwards': a line that puzzled a few male reviewers); or else she is realistic and won't snatch her sailor boy (Gig Young) 'from the cradle'. Her wry humour gets to the parts that 'bitterness doesn't stand a chance of reaching.

In short, it is one of the most sympathetic portraits that Hollywood ever drew of the unmarried woman. Whereas Miriam is the woman who should feel blessed with a family, she interprets happiness in totally material terms and can't deal with reality until she has turned it into trashy fiction. Bette is the one without husband or children, and by the end of the film has lost her young lover; yet she sees success in terms of self-fulfilment and remains a warmly outgoing and forgiving woman. While it is true that her reason for not breaking up Hopkins's marriage has its masochistic bias ('There is a certain ecstasy in wanting things you can't get'), the point is not laboured. Some male film critics who identified with Hopkins's husband (John Loder) expressed bewilderment at his not getting off with the woman who has all the virtues his own wife so patently lacks, including the virtue of loving him. Bosley Crowther wrote fretfully: 'Unless there is some strange fixation in female psychology which this reviewer does not ken, there is certainly no basis in nature for such endurance as is shown in this film.' But it would have been easier for him (and Loder) to understand Davis's hesitation had the two women, Bette and Miriam, actually been presented as the sisters (good and bad) whom they appear to be in spirit.

Despite the two decades that the film covers, Davis impeccably preserves the consistency of her character: which is not to imply that she does not change. True, she stays a faithful adherent to the same style of men's pyjama tops for thirteen years and one suspects that the grey streak that is infiltrated into her hairdo is meant to show serious dedication to the wartime Red Cross rather than to signify encroaching middle-age. But as the years go by, her diction changes: she speaks more emphatically, as if parsing the sentences for their common sense or even listening self-mockingly to what she is saying. Interestingly, she becomes more 'British' in accent as she waxes more indignant. And how those eyelids work like snow-ploughs when she hits a pile of dialogue that even she can't shift with conviction – one dismissive blink and gone forever!

On hearing from her youthful beau that he is really in love with Hopkins's daughter, Davis's face goes as flat as the light on a grey day. She seems to age months. Photographer Sol Polito – whom she had fought to have in preference to Tony Gaudio: an inexplicable choice, considering Gaudio's transcendental work on *The Letter* – holds her in a white column of self-sacrificing light against the dark wall of her apartment, like a symbolic figure on a war memorial. It helps to understand this remarkable transformation, however, to know that director Vincent Sherman interrupted the shooting as Davis starts to hear the news – then shot her reaction some considerable time later at the end of the day, when she was visibly exhausted by work. This is one brilliant example of breaking the continuity. But no sooner has the film sprung this *coup de vieille* on Bette than it instantly awards a battle point for valour. 'Bring down my Persian lamb coat,' she commands her maid. Even if lovers go, there is still life where Persian lamb is left.

But the moment in the film that swings one's sympathies fully behind her is not less effective because the huge majority of women film-goers were anticipating it already, yearning for it, even in their heart of hearts encouraging Bette to do it. Davis has many, many times recounted how the stage at Warner Bros was crowded to the roof joists with unofficial 'kibbitzers' on the day of reckoning between her and Miriam Hopkins. The camera follows her as she saunters with deceptive yet deadly calm across the living-room to Hopkins who is clad in a full-length tea gown – during wartime austerity, too! – and still emoting about her dedication to her art – 'They'll never take that away from me!' Grabbing her by the shoulder pads, Davis shakes her rival like someone lowering the level of a waste-bin, says 'Sorry' with efficient crispness, then collects the shopping she has put down to do this purgative deed and exits – invariably to a thunder of audience applause wherever the film was (or is) shown.

As the scene plays on the screen, it conceals Miriam Hopkins's last-ditch effort to delay or subvert her own come-uppance. For as Davis seized her for the first time, she deliberately went limp, making it well-nigh impossible for the shaking she so richly deserves to be administered to her. It took all Vincent Sherman's authority – he had come on the set wearing boxing gloves – to make her stiffen up and take her punishment.

Old Acquaintance, like *Now, Voyager*, was a most successful romantic projection of the image of the 'Woman Alone', offering Bette's example as comfort and inspiration for hundreds or thousands of war 'widows' who *were*

Another WARNER Triumph

BETTE DAVIS in Mr. Skeffington
at her very greatest

CLAUDE RAINS · Walter ABEL · Richard WARING · George COULOURIS · Marjorie RIORDAN · VINCENT SHERMAN

alone in the sense of not having husbands, lovers or boyfriends immediately available. As Marjorie Rosen noted, ecstasy may be conspicuously absent from the arrangements for her 'husband-less' future that Davis has to accept at the final fade-out: yet 'her character, neither bitter nor neurotic, maintains an opulent, vital and productive life-style.'

Unfortunately the same cannot be said for the last of this amazing group of wartime 'vehicles' for an actress now in the prime of life and in full command of her talents.

Mr Skeffington (1944) is like *The Little Foxes* in that it defines its heroine, Mrs Skeffington, primarily in terms of financial opportunism. Fanny Skeffington, played by Davis with a lighter-toned voice that subtracts years from her strikingly at the start but leads to 'sing-song' problems with the onset of old age, is motivated by economic insecurity to try and hook the rich Jewish banker Job Skeffington (Claude Rains). Not that the opportunism is one-sided – for Job seeks assimilation into the old, if now impoverished ruling class of the town. As things turn out, though, it is the business transaction aspect that comes out on top. It is not simply the sheer warmth of character that Rains brings to the role which tends to cast a colder than usual light on Davis. His is one of the most sympathetic and explicit portrayals of a Jew in Hollywood movies; and the understandable anxiety of the front office where the faith was historically entrenched may well have helped tip the balance of many scenes in his favour. But the film's relationship with its audience is also ambiguous. After the marriage of Job and Fanny has become a matter of separate bedrooms, and Davis has unconvincingly but mercifully briefly reverted to a *Fog over Frisco*-type of playgirl with a gangster lover in the speakeasy business – the story settles into a protracted display of several of the anxiety-states that Hollywood was by now using with baleful if profitable effect on its loyal female audiences. Having got rich, Fanny Skeffington must pay for it – by getting old.

Not ageing gracefully, either: but catching pneumonia and seeing all her hair drop out, leaving her with only a frizzy fuzz. The shot of Davis in bed with a wig on the bedside stand calls for a plaque on the lines of 'Queen Elizabeth Slept Here'. Retribution this time resides in ugliness. Fanny is reminded by her daughter, 'You haven't been beautiful since you sent my Father away.' (Mr Skeffington, showing, one might think, small sense of events for a Jewish banker, has gone off to Germany on the eve of Hitler's accession.) Women who

Below, with Col. J. L. Warner, 1943.

Opposite, widowed by the sudden death of Arthur Farnsworth, she threw herself into Hollywood's war-effort. As the presiding spirit of *Hollywood Canteen* (1944), she joined John Garfield, Jane Wyman and Jack Carson in giving out autographs.

had enjoyed seeing Bette get her just desserts in the past were now confronted with a film that seemed intent on making them uneasy about their own fate in the scheme of things. Nothing in any earlier Bette Davis film is so horrifying as the simple 'insert' shot of a patently false curl falling off Bette's hair-do and landing at the feet of an old and now hard-up ex-beau who is trying to marry her for *her* money. Meeting age with chic and chin-up had been a tremendous source of strength (and box-office) in *Old Acquaintance*: but looking like a Queen Mother reduced to the absurd plight of shedding one's locks in public turns *Mr Skeffington* into a horror film for women of a certain age. Davis does her best to retrieve the situation by quipping, 'I find that one should never look for admirers at the same time as one is falling to bits.' But it is a chilling jest.

But then the summer of 1943 was a troubled and tragic time for Bette Davis. Just before *Mr Skeffington* started shooting, and while she was in the middle of a make-up test at the studio, word reached her that her husband had collapsed on Hollywood Boulevard. Two days later, he died. As he had been engaged on classified war work in the aeronautics industry and the briefcase he had been carrying was missing – though it transpired a bystander had taken it into safe-keeping – an autopsy had to be held and added its own strain to his widow's grief. It was as starkly unexpected an event as any in a Bette Davis film script. Farnsworth's death was declared due to natural causes and she was back at work within the month. Even then, things did not go smoothly. As if shaken by her sudden widowhood, her manner became very exacting. Inter-office memos suggest a protracted and expensive series of 'difficulties' attributed, rightly or wrongly by the parties concerned, to the star's wanting to be producer and director as well. The film took five months to make and finished up sixty days over schedule and tens of thousands of dollars over budget.

Davis's strong temperament had been

accepted by Jack L. Warner in the past: after all, she had often exerted it and the film (or her part in it) had emerged improved; and Warner knew he couldn't step into his stars' shoes. But the businessman in him resented stars trying to step into *his*. Had *Mr Skeffington* been a commercial hit, all might have been forgiven: but it was not. Even critics sympathetic to Davis's sheer gall in the past dismissed it as a lesson in the wages of vanity – a tedious lesson at that. Amid the recriminations, Davis asked for a release from her contract. She met with a refusal.

Only indirectly had the war figured in the

128

films she made. Twice she entertained the troops on celluloid; once in *Thank Your Lucky Stars* (1943) singing and dancing the 'They're Either Too Young or Too Old' number; and again as the presiding spirit of *Hollywood Canteen* (1944), which emerged less as a grateful tribute to the Services than a self-congratulatory hymn to Hollywood's own entertainment values. In *Watch on the Rhine* (1943), a Lillian Hellman melodrama that artfully attracted a spurious importance to itself by playing on the conscience of a country that entered the anti-Nazi struggle late in the day, she played a patriotic refugee in Washington DC who loses her husband to the European resistance. But there was always something suspect about Davis delivering a Message in wartime. Her chosen territory was the interior one of the human emotions, not the overseas one occupied by the enemy.

In the last year of the war, a 'new' star reported for work at Warner Bros. Joan Crawford had in fact been put on the Warner pay-roll in July 1943, two days after she and MGM had dissolved a relationship that had lasted eighteen years; but she had retired to her home (and her housework) as if to a bunker, to recoup her energies, and it had taken Warner Bros nearly a year to find a property to suit the head of steam that she built up. Her first Warner Bros film, *Mildred Pierce*, won her an Oscar. Though Davis never commented on it, Crawford's presence at Warners as a strong and viable alternative to her own was a disturbing factor in the power game.

One film-maker who directed both stars, Curtis Bernhard, later said the chief difference between them was that Davis was an *actress* through and through, working towards her effects by conscious intelligence; Crawford was a very talented *motion-picture star* whose feelings took such tenacious possession of her that she was often still 'in' the part twenty minutes after 'Cut' had been called.

It is certainly Davis's intelligence which shines through *The Corn Is Green* (1945).

'They're Either Too Young or Too Old.' Davis herself was coming up to 40, the awkward age of stardom when available roles also were either too young or too old.

Directed by Irving Rapper, it was Casey Robinson's last screenplay for her: no doubt about it, this Cornell graduate, who had entered silent films as a title writer in 1927, had the measure of Davis's emotional range better than any other scenarist at Warners, and constantly used what he knew she could do to extend her means to do what she wanted to do. He refined her talent in the writing so as to feed her mind as well. The studio may have hoped that the spark of learning which her didactic school-marm ignited in her Welsh scholarship boy could be fanned into a suggestion of something warmer. Davis would have none of it. Her dedication has just the right hint of fanaticism: it is as selfless a piece of work as any she did.

But as the war reached its end, the Hollywood scene was marked by great uncertainty. Society had begun changing at a speed that surprised even a multi-billion-dollar film business geared to the rapid shifts in audience tastes. A new kind of audience seemed to come of age

Opposite, with Paul Lukas (in back seat) in *Watch on the Rhine* (1943): wartime 'messages' were not her forte.

Messages from the heart were delivered with more dedication in *The Corn Is Green* (1945). Playing a teacher suited an actress who reached for effects with conscious intelligence. 'Below, Meet the real Miss Moffat.' Emlyn Williams introduces Miss Grace Cook, the teacher he took as his model.

overnight. Teenagers taking advantage of freedom in one-parent homes, with a working mother away all day, had developed as a separate sub-group with their own part-time jobs to close the gap between pocket money and wage packet. The rise of the Pop fans, or 'bobbysoxers', alone spawned a youth culture different from – and reacting against – the Hollywood-manufactured child stars. Pop music promoted by jukeboxes helped the creation of idols like Frank Sinatra and swelled an eight-million-dollar record industry. For the first time, Hollywood had serious competition from stars who had been made outside the movie industry.

The youth market was more curious about matters not yet permitted by the film censors to be depicted on the screen, and this set Hollywood both a problem and a temptation. Neither, it was clear, was going to be solved by stars of even Bette Davis's early middle-age: she was now on the edge of forty.

Moreover, the women who had been her most loyal fans for a generation were now being disbanded as the men came back from the wars. Their female replacements in stores, offices and factories were being discharged to make way for the veterans. This mass dismissal of the patriotic regiment of women started a reluctant homeward-bound trek which has still not been adequately chronicled in American social history. Many of the five million women who entered the workforce during the first two years of the war had come to love the freedom and authority that work outside the home gave them; they did not want to return to their traditional roles as wives and mothers. Many were compelled to go back. While the American blacks derived lasting gains from the wartime suspension of segregation at work, peacetime left a bittersweet taste in the lives of women who rejoiced in the safe return of their loved ones but mourned the loss of *camaraderie* with their own sex as new labour laws were introduced or old ordinances revived to oust them from their jobs.

Hollywood, too, shifted into sexist gear. Male stars from the wars returning got preferential treatment. They still had a huge investment value to studios which wanted the profits to start flowing as soon as possible. And profits were certainly needed. The post-war box-office was dipping. Taxes were rising. And following Olivia de Havilland's victory in the Los Angeles Superior Court, in 1944, establishing that the customary seven-year Hollywood contract was akin to peonage, or serfdom, and therefore unlawful, the very movie stars could no longer be compelled to occupy a fixed place in their studio heaven.

Movies were once again addressing themselves to a man's world, and the stars of the 1930–45 period not only sensed that the production machine which sustained them was faltering for the first time since the talkies, but that no one really knew how to look after the particular product that had won so many of them, Davis included, the love and loyalty of millions – namely, the 'woman's picture'.

SLEEP MY LOVE AND PEACE ATTEND THEE,
ALL THROUGH THE NIGHT.
GUARDIAN ANGELS GOD WILL LEND THEE,
ALL THROUGH THE NIGHT.

SOFT THE DROWSY HOURS ARE CREEPING,
HILL AND VALE IN SLUMBER STEEPING,
LOVE ALONE HIS WATCH IS KEEPING,
ALL THROUGH THE NIGHT.

5

THE INDESTRUCTIBLE

THE FIVE YEARS FROM 1945 TO 1950 WERE restless, unhappy ones for Bette Davis. She was relentless and demanding at work, and usually dissatisfied with the result. Over one thing, however, she got her way at last. For a long time she had wanted to produce her own films. Now she set up her own independent corporation: Warner Bros agreed to distribute the first of her productions, *A Stolen Life* (1946).

As if there were now too many warring 'Bette Davises' to be contained in one character, she divided her role in two, playing twin sisters, identical in looks, totally different in natures, the nice one of whom survives a boating accident and, posing as her sibling, returns to the man (Glenn Ford) whom her nasty sister had seduced away. It was based on a 1939 film of the same title made in Britain by Paul Czinner and starring his wife Elisabeth Bergner (in the dual roles) with Michael Redgrave as the shared man in their lives. Davis always regretted that American censorship restrained her version from hinting as boldly as the British film that the surviving sister's life with the man who was in fact her brother-in-law extended into the bedroom. All kinds of ruses were adopted to *stop* the relationship getting too close for the censor's comfort. In her interviews at this time, Davis expressed her impatience at the hypocritical postures that the Hays Office was still forcing on the post-war American film industry. It was as if she realized that she herself had just about gone the permitted distance in movies like *The Letter, The Great Lie* and even *Old Acquaintance*, which had caused a lot of censorship heartburn on account of her middle-aged character's affair with a much younger man. (In this respect, a comparison of *Old Acquaintance* with its remake, *Rich and Famous*, directed by George Cukor in 1981, is amusing: in this post-permissive version, the Davis character [now played by Jacqueline Bisset] not only has an affair with a *Rolling Stone* journalist, but is picked up by a gigolo on Fifth Avenue who ends up very willingly in her bed at the Algonquin.) If she was to explore new

sides of herself, and open up new areas of emotional experience for the age group she was now in, then she had to have fresh ground on which to trespass. This meant censorship had to be relaxed.

For all that, *A Stolen Life* enjoyed great popularity and made her feel she was managing her professional life as she wished, but her personal life – that was something else again.

About this time she had met the man who was to become her third husband. At twenty-nine, ten years her junior, William Grant Sherry had already drifted through several casual jobs, including spells as a boxer and a male nurse. He was in his 'Sunday painter' phase when Davis, perhaps reacting against her mother's objections to what she saw as Sherry's erratic, even obstreperous nature, began an affair with him that led to their marriage late in 1945. The union endured a bare five years, but produced a daughter, Barbara, in 1947. Viewed in the retrospective light of a vituperative marriage, *A Stolen Life* casts some curious omens of its own over the future Mrs Sherry. The story was rewritten by Catherine Turney, a friend of Davis's, to impregnate it with the New England saltiness she knew would appeal to the star's outdoor nature. But it also introduced out of nowhere a maverick artist called Karnock (Dane Clark) who repays the 'nice' Bette for her encouragement of his truly terrible work with tongue-lashing abuse tempered by fierce outbursts of (verbal) passion on the lines of 'Man needs woman, woman needs man: it's that basic.' The character drops suddenly out of the story, as if his 'basicness' had landed on the cutting-room floor and stayed there; but something like this intemperate relationship appears to have been resurrected in Davis's life with Sherry. Films have an odd way of projecting on to the real life of their stars the situations they precipitate as characters on the screen. The very bait that shrewd script-writers employ to hook a star, by creating a character who is a desirable self-image, or pro-

Opposite, third marriage, in 1945, to William Grant Sherry, along with her mother and her second husband. It lasted barely five years and ended in vituperative recrimination . . . but produced a daughter, 'B.D.' for ('Barbara Davis').

Now her own producer, Davis cast Glenn Ford opposite her in *A Stolen Life* (1946), a man shared between identical twin sisters, one nice, the other nasty, both Bette Davis.

...sing a situation that appeals the star's own ...ntasies, can make the impressionable per-...nality begin to restructure his or her life that ...y, too. Not only during the period of the ...m's shooting: but when it is over as well. *A ...olen Life* has a residual feeling of being con-...ued in Davis's new life.

While searching for a property that her own ...mpany could produce, she made two more ...ms for Warner Bros – both critical and com-...ercial disappointments.

Deception (1946) reunited the *Now, Voyager* ...o of herself, Paul Henreid and Claude Rains, ...t now locked into a jealous love affair offer-...g no possibility for audiences to interact with ...e stars. *Winter Meeting* (1948: the long gap ...tween films being due to Davis's post-natal ...cuperation) could have been interesting. But ...m censorship, whose institutional basis was ...oman Catholic in origin, devitalized the ...eme of a woman's love for a man whose own ...ve for his church comes between them. Then ...me *June Bride* (1948), a well-received light ...medy, but equally light on box-office returns. ...avis starred as a New York woman's ...agazine executive re-vamping the folksy life-...yle of a smalltown family for her sophisti-...ted readership – and, in the process, learning ...ew simple virtues not taught in the big city.

She was not making much progress in find-...g material her own company could film. Two ...eas she explored were to remain perennial ...vourites – and unproduced. One was Edith ...harton's novel *Ethan Frome*; the other, a ...reen biography of Abraham Lincoln's wife ...ary, a personage with the kind of regal spine ...her that appealed to Davis. The writer Alvah ...ssie, who was to be among the 'blacklisted' ...mes in Hollywood during the 'anti-Red' ...tch-hunts, actually did a stint on the Mrs ...ncoln story, using as its basis an unpublished ...ay that Davis had commissioned, perhaps ...tending to do it on the stage. The difficulty, ...ssie reported, was ensuring it did not turn ...to the *Mr* Lincoln story. Davis saw eye to ...e with him on *that*!

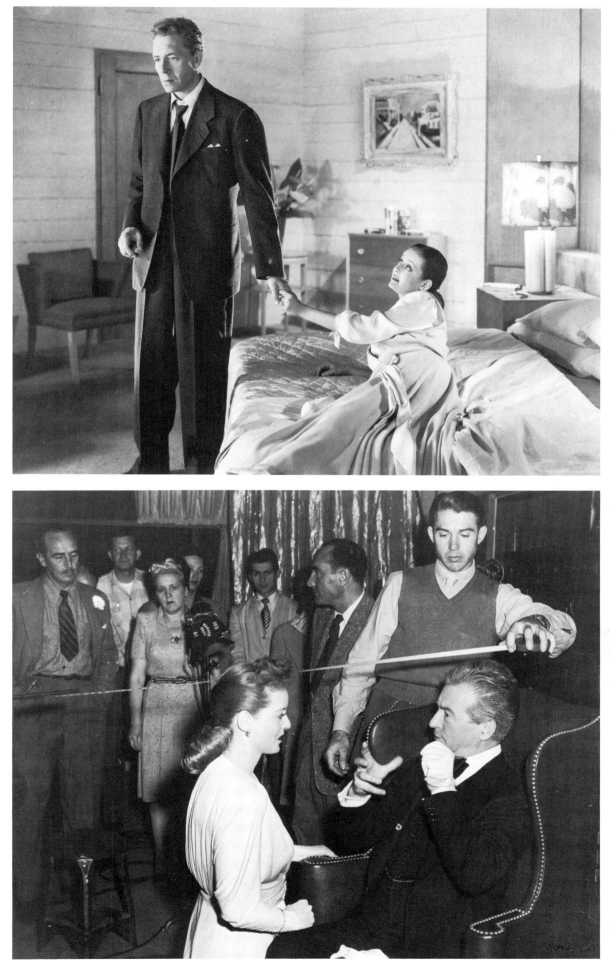

posite, a watery end
aits the bad sister:
nsorship was waiting for
e survivor, however.
ception **(1946) reunited**
e stars of *Now, Voyager*,
t locked Bette into a
lous triangle with Paul
enreid and Claude Rains
d denied the audience its
ice in the affair. Even the
ecise focus-puller
uldn't create the old close
lationship.

139

But as nothing came of her efforts to get the subject financed in 1948–49, she agreed to do *Beyond the Forest* (1949) as her next Warner picture. It turned out to be her last in their eighteen-year relationship.

In fluctuating health, with her marriage long gone to grief, Davis's portrayal of a self-destructive Wisconsin housewife who commits murder and has an abortion simply to be up and off to Chicago, where her lover and 'independence' await her, turned out to be at best an embarrassing miscalculation, at worst shocking self-parody. Looking back, one discerns that the excesses of *What Ever Happened to Baby Jane?* had their origins in this period of personal unhappiness and professional uncertainty. Rosa Moline in *Beyond the Forest* looked a caricature of Davis's screen image as some of her detractors might have seen it: even the most charitable view of it as a performance struggling against the odds to present a view of a 'liberated woman' runs into objections that it could be more plausibly interpreted as a public confession of self-hatred.

But then there seemed to be an inimical virus in the air that the woman stars breathed in the late 1940s. It drove them to take self-punishing roles that pushed the characters they played to the extremes of neurotic, even psychotic behaviour. Once the wartime focus of attention for the exemplary virtues they represented, or the cathartic experience their identifiable vices offered film-goers, they now appeared to be trying to recapture their public's interest and admiration in roles of manic hysteria. Joan Crawford in Curtis Bernhard's *Possessed*, in 1947, went mad, shot her stepdaughter's lover and ended up in a mental asylum. Olivia de Havilland was also incarcerated among the overwrought and unbalanced denizens of *The Snake Pit* in 1949. Davis's heroine in *Beyond the Forest* seemed seized by some form of dementia. She wore a wig that looked like a wriggling bunch of black snakes, cast piercing Medusa-like looks at all and sundry and, delirious from an attack of peritonitis follow-

ing her abortion, dragged herself off to the railroad station to catch the Chicago-bound train in the longest death-crawl in screen history, pausing only long enough to drag lipstick across her mouth, as if cancelling out a debt to her deadly dull marriage, and ejaculate at her maid with hungry anticipation of independence, 'Excitement, Jenny, have you never heard of excitement!' This Wisconsin Emma Bovary expires in front of the very train she hoped to take to freedom, looking for a brief, forceful moment like a victim who has been sacrificed to a steaming, hissing god.

It is a role conceived and played in continuous breakdown. Its excesses brought her the cruellest notices of her life in 1949: a reduction of her stardom to 'the realms of the absurd', as one critic put it. Even a kindlier era now regards *Beyond the Forest* as the apotheosis of Hollywood camp, having been cued to see it as such by Martha in Edward Albee's *Who's Afraid of Virginia Woolf?* who spits out the Davis line, '*What a dump!*' with

the vampire relish of someone sucking on the same vein of bitchery as Davis. (Indeed Martha and her victim-spouse George might have been created by a playwright whose pabulum was the Bette Davis movies of his childhood and adolescence.)

The film was shot in a series of confrontations between the star and the veteran director King Vidor. Vidor resisted many of Davis's suggestions. In her most inflexible mood, she went to see Jack L. Warner in the middle of shooting. It was almost as if she was carrying the self-destructive curse of Rosa Moline along with her. Reports of the meeting vary. But all agree on one thing: Warner had to choose between Davis and Vidor.

'Well, I think at that time they were very anxious to cancel her contract,' Vidor later recalled, 'so they jumped at it. They had an agreement there in ten minutes.'

Davis has denied that her brutal leave-taking happened this way. But in the subsequent interviews in which she touched on it, she didn't

absolve herself of blame. In fact, she claimed a large share of it. She recounted how she telephoned Jack L. Warner and told him that *Beyond the Forest* wouldn't get finished – it had then three days' shooting left on her scenes – unless he promised to annul her contract. She recalled that she had felt guilty about this personal 'blackmail', even after the film received its devastating reviews, until Warner's own bellicose memoirs were published. In them, he said he'd been happy to see the back of her. 'That made two of us J.L.,' she noted acidly.

On 21 October 1949, the day that *Beyond the Forest* opened in New York, Bette Davis was filing a suit for divorce from William Grant Sherry. At the court's urging, an attempt was made to patch up their discord. Sherry consulted an analyst and was given advice that sounds well ahead of its time, since he began assuming the role and obligations of a 'housewife', cleaning the house and preparing the meals. Alas, such premature role-reversal only seemed to irk a wife who still hankered for a

man who would put her in her place, instead of being her stand-in. By mid-1950, the marriage was dissolved.

Ironically, the film Davis was engaged in shooting at the time was entitled *The Story of a Divorce*, though it was changed to *Payment on Demand* (1951), hardly as apposite, since Sherry had signed a premarital waiver relinquishing all claims on his wife's estate. Directed and part-written by Curtis Bernhardt, the film played the role-reversal game, too, since it was the husband (Barry Sullivan) who held the pistol to his wife's head by demanding a divorce: which gives Davis the chance to review her marriage in flashback, then determine on revenge and bleed her ungrateful spouse white before offering to take him back again. Inside every hard woman, the film suggested, beats a soft heart. But the best scenes were the hardest-hearted: the way private investigators see other people's distress in terms of their own profit, the *angst* of dividing up the common property, the custody of the

child. . . . One doesn't know if Davis took any hand in the script: but the film feels it has absorbed the pain of some of her own life. But then, in a very real sense, she turned some of her films into essays in autobiography. She altered lines, not only to protect herself against a clumsy writer since she knew it was she who would have to carry the can, but also to extend reality (as she saw it, anyhow) into someone else's work of fiction.

But one man whose fiction she did not alter by a word – much to his surprise, as there were plenty of Davis's 'friends' to warn him of what to expect – was Joseph L. Mankiewicz, her next director, and author of a film that merged its leading character so inseparably with Davis that it seemed to have been written with her in mind from the start.

In fact she was not even the first person to be offered what became the last great film of her career – and many would say her best-known role.

When *All About Eve* (1950) was being cast, Davis was in the middle of filming *Payment on Demand* for RKO and was deemed unavailable. The film was a Twentieth Century-Fox production, and Darryl F. Zanuck's first choice had been Marlene Dietrich. Mankiewicz quickly vetoed that. He found it hard, however, to get the screenplay past the praetorian guard of agents and lawyers protecting Gertrude Lawrence, who had been his choice. So in February 1950 Claudette Colbert was signed; but she wrenched her back and had to drop out. By good luck, Davis had just finished shooting *Payment of Demand* – and inside two weeks she found herself playing Margo Channing.

Asked often in later years how Colbert's interpretation might have differed from Davis's, Mankiewicz answered that he had envisaged her Margo as a more refined bitch whose favourite weapon of retort would be the fencing foil, rather than the 'boozy slugger-from-the-toe' that Davis gave him when she growled so memorably, 'Fasten your seat belts.

143

It's going to be a bumpy night.'

After one has swallowed the initial improbability of the way that Eve (Anne Baxter), the worm in Big Apple, is accepted inside Margo Channing's 'family circle' backstage, *All About Eve* is the shrewdest, truest commentary on the 'actress personality' ever assembled on the screen. One must always be grateful that Davis, at forty, was the perfect age to play it – indeed to play herself. Not for the first time, she makes a leading role over into her own star *persona*, even though Mankiewicz insists his creation is just about every actress of note from Peg Woffington (the flamboyant eighteenth-century star of Drury Lane) to Tallulah Bankhead. Davis herself, it's often been said, used Bankhead as her model. The truth is, the husky voice resembling Bankhead's which Davis used as Margo was forced on her by a minor throat rupture just before shooting: continuity compelled her to retain the abrasive register even after the blood vessels healed.

One of the great advantages enjoyed by *All About Eve* is to have a star who is in every way as big a myth as her character. Davis's own larger than life *persona* validates Margo's, just as her film star mannerisms are skin-grafted on to Margo's Broadway style.

As the film opens it is Eve who is receiving her award from the Sarah Siddons Society; but the accent of interest is firmly placed on Davis who has already won a bigger prize than any the stage provides – namely a woman's right to a life of her own. Eve is the minion still in thrall to ambition: Margo, released from the bondage of ambition, is the woman at liberty. She is still, however, the great prowling cat of the jungle. Without stirring from her supper table, or indeed speaking a line, Davis establishes an image of a woman who is still a force to reckon with, yet no longer cares overmuch about worldly power or defeat, since her own identity has been made secure. That cigarette plucked from the lips like the pin from a grenade; that dismissive gesture to the waiter offering to water her drink which says that

she'll take it neat, as she takes life; that angular appraising glance of the ex-champ summing up the new contender; those eyes as candid as the light bulbs framing her dressing-room mirror: Davis keeps the style that has made her famous, but transmutes the substance.

The message she signals is rendered even more subtle by Mankiewicz's discernment. He puts Margo firmly on the side of the footlights where real life is lived, yet allows her to retain the mythical dimensions of the other side where make-believe exists. Just as Davis wrote of her own coming into the world in terms of theatre and high drama, Margo sees *her* whole existence on or off stage in terms of acting. Every major scene she appears in is written and performed outsize – like a play. Although Mankiewicz made his own career in Hollywood, his sympathy lay, like Davis's, firmly to the east of it, in the same theatrical milieu where his star first tasted the transcendent experience of being (as she wrote) 'alone . . . on stage and everywhere'. Margo Channing is surely what Bette Davis would have become had she not gone to Hollywood. Small wonder that she declared it was one of the easiest roles she'd ever played. When her baby had been born a few years earlier, she had joyfully exclaimed that she had 'both Hollywood *and* family'. After *All About Eve*, she might have added '. . . *and* Broadway'.

The title *All About Eve* is a wilful misdirection: there really isn't all that much to tell about Eve, except a rather grubby secret that will keep her in thrall to an even lower species of Broadway life than that of an apprentice who steals her mistress's role – namely, the theatre critic Addison DeWitt (George Sanders) who exposes her deceit. About Margo Channing, on the other hand, there is *everything* to learn – and Davis partakes of self-knowledge at the same time as she satisfies our greedy appetites. In particular she learns what it is to come to terms with the one enemy she can't out-act – age. The whole screenplay is conceived with this universal truth in mind: it

is about the sole truth Broadway recognizes, and the film underlines it again and again. The unfairness of age, when men continue to look younger than they are, while women don't; Lloyd the playwright (Hugh Marlowe) longing to have a leading lady 'of the right age' in the role he's written; Bill the director (Gary Merrill) who puts the knife into Margo and twists it every time he calls Eve 'a kid'; even Addison DeWitt snidely using his column to chide (without naming) 'actresses [who] continue playing roles requiring a youth and vigour of which they retain but a dim memory.' In short, the court circle is telling Margo what she won't recognize in her make-up mirror. She comes to terms with age just about the time that Davis herself was doing so in real life. If ever there was a role that found its interpreter at a time that was ripe for both of them, this is it.

The moment Davis accepts that fact in the film is a poignant one. After her magnificent gale-force outburst in the empty theatre at friends' betrayal which has allowed Eve to sneak in and grab the role of understudy, Margo's anger blows itself out as Bill, her director, holds her down on a bed on the stage set, her face in the first stage of transition from the picture of Mrs Siddons as 'The Comic Muse' which hangs in her apartment to the 'Tragic Muse' that acknowledges the onset of the menopausal years. Pinning her to the bed by strength and emotion, Bill asks her to marry him – and for the first and only time in the film, Margo falters. Bill asks, 'Tell me, what's behind all this?' and she replies in a whimper, 'I – I don't know, Bill. Just a feeling. I don't know.' She is left alone, piteous, in long shot.

But in the film's 'last act', her regenerative strength produces a quieter wisdom than the terrors of middle-age that Hollywood habitually heaped on stars whose looks (and box-office appeal) were slipping. Her acceptance of marriage is not a sell-out, though: simply a re-adjustment. Henceforth, she will play 'grown-up women only, I might even play a mother – only one child of course, and not over eight.'

Flying off or flying in: the new marriage looked made to last.

Opposite the family circle enlarged: 'B.D.' joined by an adopted daughter named 'Margot' (with a 't') after the *All About Eve* character: a boy was also adopted. Temperament will out in public, however: and the inevitable *paparazzo* was there to record it.

It is a disarming example of how to keep your cake and eat it, too: but film-goers are hypnotized into seeing this talented, self-centred woman now settling for the imperfect lives that most of them lead – and they love Davis all the more for seeming to retire so gracefully among them. Margo is in this sense a sort of Everywoman: in all other senses, she remains Bette Davis.

Davis and Anne Baxter were both nominated for the 'Best Actress' Oscar – the first time such a 'double' had been brought off by one film – and presumably each knocked the other out at voting time, since the award that year went to Judy Holliday as the dumb blonde in *Born Yesterday*.

However, Davis had already acquired one memento of the film. Like Margo, she married her Bill. Her divorce from William Grant Sherry became final on 4 July 1950, and just over three weeks later Gary Merrill became her fourth husband. They adopted a five-year-old child and named her Margot. There is an eerie feeling here of stars continuing to play the script after the final fade-out. Indeed in later years it seemed to Davis that Merrill had fallen in love with *the character* she played and imagined he was getting Margo Channing as his wife!

Davis was now a freelance actress. There was no studio to support her career, to select scripts, supervise rewrites, surround her with publicity and all the high-profile appurtenances of stardom. Producers desiring to hire her for her name and talent were not always the ones with the money to back them. On the contrary: *she* was the collateral on which they endeavoured to borrow the budget. Unless she was astute or lucky, 'independence' was much more hazardous; not every star who sought to enjoy it discovered that he or she had the acumen to manage it. *All About Eve* was a film with no heirs: it was not followed by a flood of offers. *Payment on Demand*, though shot before it, was released four months after it. The long delay had given Howard Hughes, who

controlled RKO, time to change his mind about the ending – and have *it* changed. Formerly, she had ended the movie as a lonely but uncompromising *divorcee*: in the new, softer ending, she was required to give the impression that she just *might* take her husband back again. It galled her to have to settle for a points victory when she had already won the game fair and square for her own sex.

Critics praised her nuanced performance: but coming after her incandescent Margo, it seemed to some critics, who were ignorant of the order in which the two films were shot, that she was back in a formula. One of the strengths of *All About Eve* was that it had definitely not been 'a Bette Davis vehicle'. Hers wasn't even the largest part in it: simply the largest ego. The egalitarian distribution of the roles is one reason for the film's popularity.

From 1951, she and her new husband made a series of bad career decisions, starting with a film they made together in England. *Another Man's Poison* (1951) cast her as a neurotic murderess in the fen country who poisons her blackmailing spouse (Merrill) and a suspicious friend before the local vet (Emlyn Williams) tries to revive her from a fainting fit by a glass of the same fatal liquid. Nothing could save the film from being box-office poison.

Next she grasped the acting opportunities offered by the role of a stoic widow in *Phone Call from a Stranger* (1952), which starred her husband and had Shelley Winters heading the cast after proving herself in *A Place in the Sun*. Davis's billing – eleventh in the cast – created the impression less of a generous actress than of a slipping star. Her next film, *The Star* (1953), wasn't released till almost a full year later: where once she had two or three films a year, now she had barely one – and that a poor one.

The Star gives the impression of a new kind of film trying to escape from an old formula. It was shot on real locations in and around Hollywood; but its up-to-date sense of actuality is at odds with the histrionic masochism of a fallen star. It has pretensions to be a West Coast *All About Eve*, but its true antecedent is *Sunset Boulevard*, made two years earlier. The film star played by Davis is too old for the roles that stardom needs to feed on and makes what she hopes is a successful test for a 'come-back' film. In the best scene, played by Davis with unsparing candour, she witnesses the pathetic truth about herself when she sees the test screened. Even then she refuses to admit she has lost her throne and drives drunkenly around Beverly Hills with an Oscar she once won (actually the one Davis received for a not dissimilar role in *Dangerous* eighteen years earlier) perched like a gremlin on the dashboard. Davis's flailing performance won praise. Bosley Crowther wrote in the *New York Times*: 'Violently, she represents the fury and the vengeance of an actress whose career has come to a point of grim transition while she herself will not acknowledge change.' All that was wrong with that was that some people felt it applied to Davis, too. Ironically, that had also been Gloria Swanson's fate. Just because Swanson's evocation of fallen greatness in *Sunset Boulevard*, was so powerful, many filmgoers actually believed she had failed in the talkies and had been living in a state of reclusive trauma ever since! *The Star* was a brave film, but definitely bad timing.

After it, the mistakes multiplied. She turned down the role Shirley Booth later played opposite Burt Lancaster in *Come Back Little Sheba*: 'One of the really great mistakes of my career.'

Then, as if *All About Eve* had touched off her nostalgia, she decided to do a Broadway show – and made an erratic choice. It is ironical that when Elizabeth Taylor, likewise seeking to re-route a career that had lost direction, appeared on Broadway thirty years later, she chose *The Little Foxes* and the part of Regina which had been one of Davis's biggest film successes. Davis might have been wiser to trust the maxim that the public like what they know and to select a melodrama with a strong appeal to

149

Phone Call from a Stranger (1952), left: deep waters, a shallow part.

Below, the star meets *The Star* (1953), a film shadowed by the recognition, on screen and in life, of an actress facing up to the point of grim transition in her career . . but still capable of giving a flailing performance.

AUCTION TO·NIGHT
PERSONAL EFFECTS
OF
MARGARET ELLIOT
FAMOUS MOTION PICTURE STAR

women. Instead, ever daring to hang herself, she chose to do a series of songs, dance numbers and impersonations in a show called *Two's Company*. Though audiences appreciated her boldness, she sensed a vague unfriendliness among theatre people: it was as if some of them resented her 'going Broadway' the way the most talented of their own number had 'gone Hollywood'. It was probably not a good idea, either, to use her impersonations (of Jeanne Eagels, and others) to make fun of movie figures as well as her own Hollywood past. Ordinary people had an emotional investment in Bette Davis the screen star: there was a risk of dissipating their capital.

The show's premature closure, in March 1953, had nothing to do with bad business, however. A toothache complaint turned out to be osteomyelitis of the jaw. It put her into hospital for an immediate operation and a painful recuperation.

For the rest of that year and part of 1954, she and her family, who now included an adopted boy named Michael, stayed in Maine. Her favourite dwelling place pumped new vigour back into her: but it was as well that her next role required her to look twenty years older than she was. *The Virgin Queen* (1955) was

151

Queen Elizabeth reigns again: *The Virgin Queen* **(1955) rests up between takes.**

Below, the vulnerable years: a fan intervenes in the location shoot on *Storm Center* **(1956). And on the set of** *The Catered Affair* **(***Wedding Breakfast* **in Britain: 1956), a star becomes a character player now that character players have become the new stars of television.**

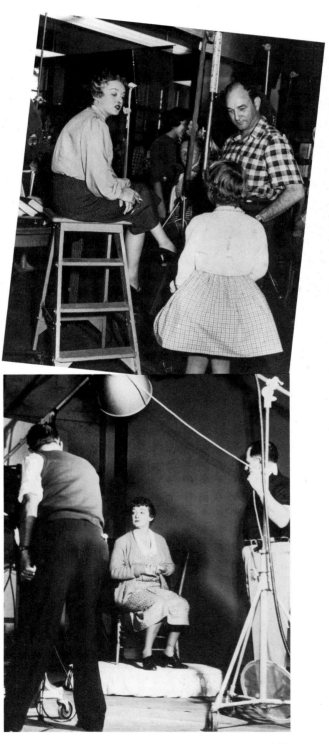

Elizabeth Tudor re-visited by a woman in the period when stardom shades into character acting. She still went the limit – and even over it. The maximum 'exposure' when she first played Elizabeth had been a 'balding' hairline: now Perc Westmore manufactured a rubber cap to simulate a completely bald cranium. Other stars let their hair down in the big parts: Bette Davis typically cut hers off – or so it looked. Even more peculiar was the regal walk she adopted, something between a strut and a hop, suggesting she had a third leg under her crinoline. But whether she was good or bad hardly mattered in a silly film turning on the Queen's learning that Sir Walter Raleigh (Richard Todd) had fitted out his cabin with a double-bed – an affront to England's honour that lands him in the Tower, only to be pardoned in time to catch the tide for the New World, with Joan Collins (future star of a Dynasty more popular than the Tudors) all pert and prettified on board. Elizabeth watches through a telescope as they sail away, in one of history's great unrecorded moments of voyeurism.

The film was a disappointment. Twentieth Century-Fox had no confidence in it. Would the public want a historical pageant? Would it be worth spending the money to make them want one? In both cases, the answer was No. What the American public wanted, in fact, was on their television sets. And as CinemaScope, VistaVision and the other novelty wide-screen formats failed as counter-attractions, Hollywood began taking risks with stories that the cautious TV networks avoided. Davis's next film, *Storm Center* (1956), was supposed to be just such an audacious 'issue' film. But the trouble was, the supposedly 'hot' issue it dealt with – bigotry, book-burning and witch-hunting in small-town America – was pretty cold by the time it went into production. 'McCarthyism' had burnt itself out years earlier; and book-burning only made for a preachy tract. Davis's portly pillar of liberty as the local librarian who sets her face against intolerance looked a lonely one, too.

Far more impact was made by the movie that followed *Storm Center* into production, though it reached the screen earlier.

The Catered Affair (1956, also known as *Wedding Breakfast* in Britain) was Davis's transition film: the bridge between her resigned glamour in *All About Eve* and her entry into undisguisedly 'older woman' roles without (as yet) the full 'hag treatment'. As a working-class housewife in her early fifties, with a Bronx-Irish accent one could plaster on the walls, a full-moon face and a solid body planted on well-worked feet, she manifested all the aches and consolations of a recognizable individual. She recalled Anna Magnani – but a Magnani reared in captivity. The film was directed by Richard Brooks from a Paddy Chayefsky play which Gore Vidal had adapted, and it showed television's influence not only in its intimate scale, but in the street-realism of its casting. Character actors were now parlour stars to the home viewers, so movie stars had to become character actors. Davis was ready – and able. Chayefsky's vernacular but skilfully selective dialogue disciplined not only her tongue, but her whole demeanour, battening down her larger-than-life mannerisms till she fitted the *petit bourgeois* conventions of a class which starves itself to put on a show of material well-being for the neighbours. At the end, when the slap-up wedding breakfast she's decreed shall take place, instead of the quiet affair her daughter wanted, has come and gone (and taken fifteen years of her husband's savings), she turns to her bedroom mirror to face an empty future. Twisting her hair into bedtime plaits, Davis lets her hands say it all like signals for the deaf – no words needed.

From the mid-1950s, her 'old' films were being shown regularly on television and she enjoyed the new lease on the past they gave her. She probably wished she could have enjoyed some percentage share in them too: but stars, with few exceptions, owned no part of their pictures unless their own companies had produced

them, and Davis, as we have seen, had not been a conspicuous success in managing her career. She found compensation in making television pay her direct. From now on, she appeared on it ubiquitously and sometimes indiscriminately in half-hour plays done 'live', in 'pilots' made for series (that often never materialized), in innumerable 'special guest' spots on chat shows. The fees were quickly consumed by the obligations which had driven her to take the work in the first place: especially sad was the discovery that her adopted daughter was badly retarded and would need expensive remedial care for the rest of her life as child and adult.

Part of the price for making ends meet was the cameo role she took as Catherine the Great in the historical potboiler *John Paul Jones* (1959), which represented the eponymous father of American sea-power being given 'bed and boat' by the Empress of Russia. 'A sad comedown' was the general verdict: but at least it cost her only two day's work and she got $55,000.

The Scapegoat (1959) followed, made in England, directed by Robert Hamer, with Davis cast as a bed-ridden, cigar-smoking, morphine-addicted French countess in a Daphne du Maurier plot about an Englishman (Alec Guinness) assuming the identity and destiny of his blueblooded French double. Davis later said she wished a 'double' could have done *her* work for her: a few baroque touches apart, it held negligible interest for her. Sad that after a lifetime's yearning to play with English actors of distinction (and Guinness was an international star, too, following his Oscar for *River Kwai* the year before), it should all have been such a let-down due to a disorganized script and that fact the Hamer was dying from alcoholism.

But the truth was also that Davis was unable to get a purchase on a career she felt slipping away from her. Her fourth marriage was none too secure, either. Gary Merrill and she took to the stage in 1959 in a recital of Carl Sandburg's poetry. At first the audiences gratified

154

poet and players. But Davis and Merrill fell out in mid-tour, and when he retired from the show, Sandburg's verse alone was no compensation for the audience's disappointment in not finding the husband-and-wife team who had given the evening a sense of privileged intimacy and completeness. On the tour across America, however, Davis was introduced to the infectious enthusiasm of audiences for a woman older than many of their own mothers. She discovered the 'youth audience', created by her old movies on television. As her movie career lost momentum, it was being turned into a powerful consolation – a cult.

A year later, in 1961, when she appeared on stage again in *The Night of the Iguana*, she had to have her entrance brought nearer and nearer the start of the play, otherwise the production was halted for several minutes by a storm of applause when she appeared. Eventually Tennessee Williams arranged for her virtually to 'take a bow' as herself before assuming the character of Maxine and proceeding with the play. It was to be a familiar pattern. Even when she had only a subsidiary role in a film or a television special, she eclipsed the nominal star in the amount of media interest she aroused. If the star was plastic jewellery, she was treated as a national heirloom. It did not displease her.

She carried the will to dominate into maturity and beyond with unimpaired vigour. But now there was a melodramatic heightening of her characteristics that unsettled many. Make-up played an even weightier part than usual: not to hide the ravages of time, but to emphasize them defiantly. *A Pocketful of Miracles* (1961) enticed her back to Hollywood which, predictably, she took to only a little less coldly than she did to Glenn Ford, who allegedly referred to the film as 'Bette's comeback'. It was a remake by Frank Capra of his 1933 comedy *Lady for a Day*. But the Runyonesque fable of an old wino woman transformed into a *grande dame* by the kindness of racketeers now felt like a hangover of the same Depression it had once helped cure. Davis spared herself no wrinkle, eye-bag or sagging chin as Annie the Bowery bug with hair like steel wool and a complexion (as a character said) that a woodpecker wouldn't deign to sink its beak in. Her life-long fascination with dual roles or 'changeling' parts supplied the film with its sole source of energy. All the same, it was a mistake to encourage her to play for sympathy – why sweeten what is already candy?

To some extent, every star of a certain age lives upon her past: but Davis made a cannibals' banquet out of hers when presented

155

Preparing to bring art to the people: the Merrills and the works of Carl Sandburg: the people turned out to hear the stars (1959–60).

In *The Night of the Iguana* (1961–62), opposite: her entrance had to be brought forward so that audiences would let the play get started.

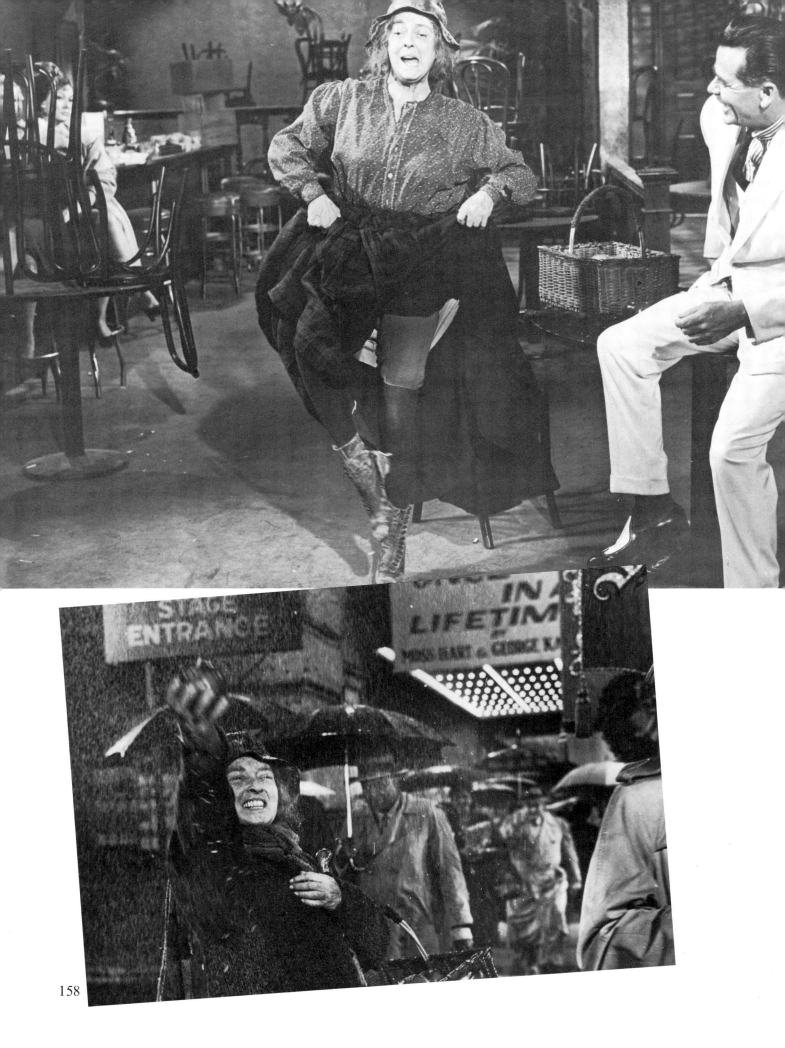

Still frisky, opposite, as Apple Annie in *A Pocketful of Miracles* **(1961). She never minded emphasizing the ravages of time; but it was the film that looked its age.**

Below, two of the greatest stars prepare to make a cannibal's banquet out of their Hollywood pasts (and, fans hoped, out of each other) in *What Ever Happened to Baby Jane?* **(1962).**

with the chance in *What Ever Happened to Baby Jane?* (1962).

Robert Aldrich had first sent the novel on which it was based to Joan Crawford. Crawford instantly cast herself as the passive, put-upon sister of Baby Jane, settling for a plethora of sympathy after a lifetime surfeit of suffering. She mentally cast Davis as her sadistic sibling who required only a broomstick to go straight into a Charles Addams cartoon. *Baby Jane* itself fed on the sort of necrophilia that was meat and drink to Addams's family of ghouls – namely the public's fascination with the movie stars of yesterday (which the Davis and Crawford characters had been) who have become today's mental cases. The two stars not only lent themselves to the film's misogynist exploitation; but since their characters were condemned to live in vengeful propinquity to each other in an Old Dark House that made the film feel like a sequel to *Psycho* two years before, the real-life stars seemed imprisoned in a Hollywood *huis clos*, an anteroom to hell,

paying for their iniquitous pasts by mutual torment of each other. The sense of mordant autobiography gave a 'B' picture the interest of a mortuary autopsy where the 'body' is a distorted but recognizable parody of the 'life'. To suggest how Baby Jane's Hollywood career had flopped a decade or two earlier, Aldrich actually used clips from two of Davis's earlier Warner Bros films, *Ex-Lady* and *Parachute Jumper*, both made in 1933, and the latter co-starring Joan Crawford's ex-husband Douglas Fairbanks Jr!

Davis insisted on doing her own make-up. It was arguably the ghastliest seen on a female face since 1935, when Dr Frankenstein created a consort for his monster. Face peeling like the distempered layers of a mildewed wall, mouth looking as if it were made up afresh each day with a cut-throat razor, eyes resembling stewed onions and hair incongruously hanging down in babyish ringlets: she looked as if she were playing Mr Punch to Crawford's long-suffering Judy. At moments such as the time she does a ferociously good imitation of Crawford on the telephone, Davis turned herself into a maliciously funny gargoyle: but more often one experienced the shock that she had reportedly incurred on seeing the completed film for the first time at the Cannes Festival. Unprepared for the cumulative effect of what she had hitherto viewed in post-synchronized fragments, Davis saw a creature who looked bottled as well as pickled. Aldrich, at her side, heard 'this quiet but kind of desperate sobbing. . . . "I just look awful," she wept. "Do I really look that awful?"'

But her performance has a small, pathetic echo that owed nothing to Aldrich's unpleasant incitement of two stars to act women on their worst behaviour. It comes to an end, when Baby Jane is discovered like a female Lear, totally out of her wits, skipping like a little girl lost along the Malibu seafront. The sheer gracefulness of her antics adds an eerie touch of its own to her mental dissolution. The ballet rhythms that Davis had learnt forty

'Do I really look that awful?' she cried when she first saw *Baby Jane*, opposite.

Below, left, Director Robert Aldrich (left) sets up a scene for *Baby Jane*: shot cheaply, it made a fortune. Davis insisted on doing her own make-up (right). Who knew it better? Bette's Baby Jane reverts to crazed childishness: Crawford's crippled sister settles for passive suffering.

On the set, opposite, Bette does a party piece with the child who played Baby Jane's younger (and saner) self.

Below, Oscar night encounter with Shirley Temple back in the 1930s, a time when it was believed child stars did not grow up to be Baby Janes like Bette.

years earlier at Roshanara's hands were serving their turn again.

Despite her marital troubles, divorce from Merrill and bitter custody battles for their adopted son, and then the death of her mother in 1962, Davis's attitude to the world was not 'Am I ready to face it?' but 'Is it ready to face me?' Her defiance was shown in a tongue-in-cheek way when she placed an advertisement in a Hollywood trade paper in September 1962. Under the heading 'Situations Wanted, Women Artists', and beside a picture of herself, it read: 'Mother of three – 10, 11 & 15 – divorcée, American. Thirty years experience as an actress in motion pictures. Mobile still and more affable than rumour would have it. Wants steady employment in Hollywood (Has had Broadway). Bette Davis, c/o Martin Baum G.A.C. References upon request.' *Baby Jane*'s success made sure no one took the joke too seriously; and as she had, for the first time in someone else's production, a substantial percentage in the box-office, she didn't need the money either.

Work was no problem: but finding work of quality *was*. She was now in the 'remakes and sequels' stage of stardom. *Dead Ringer* (1964: also known in Britain as *Dead Image*) recapitulated the plot of *A Stolen Life*, with Davis as identical twins, one of whom in this age of diminished censorship now *murdered* her sibling. But once installed in the luxury she has usurped, she finds she hasn't bargained for not knowing how to open the safe where her jewellery is locked, or having to give up her beauty sleep in order to learn to forge her sister's signature, or even discovering that along with another's affluence she acquires a gigolo (Peter Lawford) whose blackmailing is ended only when the Doberman Pinscher chews him up on the Axminster. Never were widow's needs blacker than Davis's, never was the Warner Bros corps of violins shriller. She entered full-bloodedly into the nonsense, and with the help of trick photography and a strategically sited double was able to bitch herself to her own face and even unzip the back of her twin images' evening gown – a facility that many single-image women in the audience must have envied her for. Absurd, but compulsively watchable. A judgement that recalled a remark Davis is said to have passed about her co-star in another film: 'You were really very good: you even held the audience's attention when I was off the screen.' Eugene Archer wrote: 'Deadly as her films are, Bette Davis, the star, is very much alive.'

That needs qualifying. In her own pictures, left to her own style, she was an asset however bad the movie. In other people's pictures, she tended to be a more questionable quantity – adding ripeness to badness in a pulp melodrama like *Where Love Has Gone* (1964), where her imperious dowager's uppity observation, 'Somewhere along the line, the world has lost all its standards and all its taste,' was taken down by critics the world over and used in evidence against her. Her shameless excuse was that she had made such a vulgar film to pay for her daughter's marriage. B. D.

163

Davis had married Jeremy Hyman, a relative of the Hyman clan which had bought her old *alma mater*, Warner Bros, and thus, for the brief time the studios were in their possession, allowed Davis to feel that the battlefield of her greatest successes and defeats had passed into her family.

Because *Baby Jane* had been so popular, a rematch between Davis and Crawford was attempted under the title *Hush, Hush . . . Sweet Charlotte* (1964). But illness forced Crawford to drop out, and Davis, who had star approval, gave the nod to Olivia de Havilland after Vivien Leigh had flinched from partnering her in a tale of putative parricide. Delectably demented by a suspicion that she had chopped her father's head off in childhood, Davis correctly judged the mix of gruesomeness and *gouaillerie*. Partnered by Agnes Moorehead as a crone-like servant, they looked like two of the Weird Sisters doing a bit of 'moonlighting' in Southern swampland rather than on a blasted heath. They made de Havilland look a teeny

Opposite, stardom in the 'remakes and sequels' stage. *Dead Ringer* (1964) recapitulated the 'identical twins' plot of *A Stolen Life* eighteen years earlier: only now more lenient censorship allowed 'nice' Bette to murder 'nasty' Bette. Even Paul Henreid (in dark jacket) and faithful cameraman Ernest Haller (in straw hat) were around to guide Bette's steps through a graveyard location.

Below, reunion that didn't happen: flanked by Davis and Crawford, Aldrich announces his two '*monstres sacrés*' are to star together again in *Hush, Hush . . . Sweet Charlotte* (1964). But Crawford had to drop out, pleading illness, Bette nodded approval to Olivia de Havilland as replacement – seen in script conferences with Bette and Aldrich, bottom left.

ight, Bette still at the top of the stairs in *Sweet Charlotte*.

165

Trusty retainer or covert killer? *The Nanny* (1965) turned
out a surprisingly subtle exercise in chamber horror.
Opposite, Baby Jane mutated into Mary Poppins (or
almost).

bit miscast: she struck a discordant note of
sanity.

Though the film did well and brought in the
usual shoal of offers (mostly carbon copies), it
crystallized Davis's dilemma: how long could
one go on playing freaks in order to keep one's
clawhold on the top ranks of the cast list?

When she flew to England to make *The
Nanny* (1965), the omens didn't look encouraging. For Hammer Films, the producers, had a
reputation as the 'House of Horror' which had
resurrected Dracula and reconstructed Victor
Frankenstein's monster. It hardly made one
anticipate what turned out to be the last film
role of length, craft and subtlety that Davis has
played. It is, to be sure, an exercise in *petit
guignol*: but it had a marvellous balance in the
teasing ambiguity over whether Davis, the
eponymous nursemaid, is a trusty retainer or
a covert family menace biding her time. She
even profited from Hammer's reputation as a
ghoul-raiser. For if she was *one*, then her stout
shoes, belted mackintosh, starched cuffs, pull-
on felt hat and matronly curls were the best disguise she had ever put on. The way some com-
positions are chamber music, this was chamber
horror.

It was refreshing to see Davis restrained to
the point of self-effacement as she busied herself around the English household where one
child has already died in mysterious circumstances that might (or might not) be blamed
on her. Not a hint that the perambulator she
trundles in Kensington Gardens might be a
coffin; never a second's apprehension as she
does the rounds of the night nursery that she
might be there to suck blood. Baby Jane has
been muted into Mary Poppins. As we wait for
the shriek of horror that will surely crack the
bathroom mirror, Davis emits the most chilling
sotto voce effect of a career not noted for undertones – a choking *basso profundo* that sounds
like the bath-sponge is stuck in her throat.
Director Jimmy Sangster's screenplay had the
inner logic that genuine creepiness feeds on.
For the reality of Davis's character relies on

166

Back to the grotesque gallery: maternal dragon in *The Anniversary* (1968). In the right mood, she would chop off one's head and sell it for a door-stop.

'I rob banks': as a superannuated 'Bonnie' in *Bunny O'Hare* (1971), opposite, and with Michael Redgrave in *Connecting Rooms* (1971): stars trying on old parts like old clothes.

the English upper-class heartlessness which employs a nanny to care for children whom the parents hadn't time for, while simultaneously depriving *her* of the joy of mothering any offspring of her own. If a meat cleaver was the weapon Davis had been suspected of wielding in *Sweet Charlotte*, then the tuning fork controlled her performance in *The Nanny*. Her own perfect pitch set the film vibrating.

The Anniversary (1968), also made in England for Hammer Films, took her to the opposite extreme. It was back to the Charles Addams grotesques as a ravening den-mother who turns an anniversary celebration into a series of ritual family sacrifices. She played with only one eye visible: the other was hidden, behind a baroque eyepatch (when it was not hidden, that is, under a pillow in order to frighten her pregnant daughter-in-law into a miscarriage). At least her cock-eyed look complemented the crazed relish with which she wolfed it all down. Shamelessness became Davis, in an odd way, as much as subtlety. One indignantly thinks, 'There can be no excuse for this!' – and then realizes no excuse is being offered or needed. Davis in the mood would chop one's head off and sell it for a doorstop: but who would not sacrifice his head for her?

Anyway, luridness was preferable to a lacklustre affair like *Connecting Rooms* (1971), another British film, which starred her with Sir Michael Redgrave. He played an ex-public schoolmaster wrongfully dismissed on homosexual grounds; Davis played a street entertainer falsely claiming to be a concert orchestra cellist. The feeling of stars trying on old roles like old clothes, and finding they'd seen better days, impregnated the film. Redgraves's palsied performance recalled the tight-lipped pathos of his failed schoolmaster in *The Browning Version* twenty years earlier; and Davis's past glory was suggested in the blundering in-joke of having her busk a line of London theatre-goers with a poster in the background for a play starring one 'Margot Channing'. One's only reaction is to imagine

the *sturm und drang* that the original Margo would have called down on the illiterates who had so misspelled her billing!

There was now a wildness about Davis's choice of film roles that suggests her main interest was work in any form – if not quite at any price. How else to explain *Bunny O'Hare* (1971), in which she played a superannuated 'Bonnie' to Ernest Borgnine's pensionable 'Clyde', bouncing about on the pillion of his motor-bike as both of them charged around the backwoods robbing banks? At least in *Death on the Nile* (1978) she travelled first-class. As Agatha Christie's abrasive-tongued American matron, a black pearl on a string of suspects, she filled the space between high chic and high camp, with a neck bandeau worn like a hangman's noose and a hat that looked as if it had been fashioned from an entire vulture's plumage – it *perched* rather than sat on her, determined to beat her to the swoop.

But if she had nerve for anything, physical stamina was now eluding her. In 1974, she had

In *Madam Sin*, opposite, a TV movie: scoring off the role was sometimes the only defence against having to play it.

Below, first-class travel again: Davis (seated second from right) with co-stars including Peter Ustinov and David Niven in *Death on the Nile* (1978). Jane Fonda presenting Bette Davis with Life Achievement Award in 1977: almost forty years earlier, co-star Henry Fonda has rushed off the set of *That Certain Woman* to the hospital for his daughter's birth.

embarked on the challenging venture of returning to the live stage in a musical version of *The Corn Is Green*, re-titled *Miss Moffat*, directed by Joshua Logan. But she was now 65, out of training and suffering from nerves, tensions and the return of old aches and pains. She had to withdraw. What hurt even more was the fact that the show had been sold out for months, largely on the promise of her presence in it. 'Exposure' was now the name of her tactics; for she was well aware that audiences came to see *her* – and she accepted roles on television that were sometimes improved by the expertness she brought to them. Her refusal to hide her fading looks now stood her in good stead: she used her ravaged appearance as much to score off the role as to play it. In the television film *Strangers* (1979) she had one moment that

And now, Walt Disney's turn: with Christopher Lee in
Return from Witch Mountain **(1980).**

Three generations: with daughter 'B.D.' now Mrs Jeremy Hyman, and a grandson.

was as surprising as a lava squirt from a volcano that had seemingly banked its fires. She and Gena Rowlands played a mother and daughter, long estranged and still on awkward terms when Rowlands arrives home to seek a reconciliation. She tells her mother she is dying from cancer and has not long to live. One waits for the warm human sympathy: what one gets instead is a shocking message to the contrary delivered with all Davis's intimidating combination of wrath and volume. She rejects her daughter the way a body rejects an attempt to transplant an alien organ. Monstrous: but magnificently effective.

Bizarrely now, as she entered her seventies, Bette Davis encountered crises that echoed some of the emotional traumas that scriptwriters had long ago fabricated for her talents on the screen. How exactly she played them now that they were real it would be inappropriate to speculate. But she saw her sister Barbara, whose mental and physical infirmities she had helped her sustain all her life, now coming to

her with the news that she was dying of cancer: this time there was no rejection scene. A little later, Davis herself was stricken by the same affliction and underwent an massive mastectomy. She was compelled to drop out of the role of the haughty *patronne* she had been playing in small but acid doses in the mini-series *Hotel* and noted, with ironical amusement, that the star added to the mini-series as a replacment was none other than Anne Baxter, her one-time nemesis in *All About Eve*. After the operation, she willed up her residual energy and, though plucked and wasted in appearance, resumed her predatory perch as guest star in an Agatha Christie television film, *Murder by Mirrors*.

The next blow was less tangible, but possibly more wounding: an alleged account of 'life with mother' published in 1985 by her daughter B. D. Hyman. The writer, whose sole claim to attention was her own parent's stardom and reputation, professed to be in search of the peace that confession brings. To some critics,

Mother Goddam turning into Mother Courage: at seventy-six, she moved back to Hollywood. The chair beside her may be empty, but her two Oscars claim the mantlepiece: all that matters now is work.

her endeavours seemed inspired by the prospect of other rewards than the spiritual. Davis had been pondering a second volume of her own memoirs – the first had appeared in 1962 under the stoic title *The Lonely Life* – and few doubted that the sequel would pack plenty of punch or that 'Mother Goddam' was still capable of delivering it.

'Mother Goddam . . .' She had obligingly stuck that nickname on herself to please the people who wanted to see her as the archetypal screen bitch: but really 'Mother Courage' more aptly characterizes the quality of a woman who had kept a career going for over fifty years in the cruellest as well as the most gratifying medium known to man and woman.

It would be easy and just to call Bette Davis a 'Hollywood immortal': but it is a description that suggests she has been embalmed. The choicer term which recalls the battles she has been through is a 'Hollywood indestructible'.

Bette Davis is one of the few, the very few stars who can rely on their own existence as artists even when age or inactivity has stopped them performing. She was there, in people's memories, whether or not she was there on the screen.

She impressed her durable image on the public consciousness, as well as on more than ninety cinema roles, largely as a battler for her own sex long, long before the feminists took to arms and stormed the chauvinist ramparts with banners proclaiming 'Liberation!' Not that Davis quite saw it that way: in her fight for self-assertion, she didn't need an army of women behind her. She wanted that prize for herself, so as to exercise and stretch her talents as an actress, rather than raise the status of her sex. But judged by her wider influence, she was an involuntary pioneer in this feminist area too. If this study of her 'will to action' has one dominant feature, it is the extent and duration of her reaction against the way that women like herself were mistreated by the Hollywood male hierachy of her time. Discipline went whip-in-hand with grooming. Davis endured her share

173

December, 1981: at the Los Angeles Music Center, she joins in paying tribute to Elizabeth Taylor (whose own tribute, in a way, was to revive the Davis role in *The Little Foxes*). Front row: Maureen Stapleton, Taylor, Davis, Julie Harris. Standing behind: John Warner (then Taylor's husband), Roger Moore, Gregory Peck, Roddy McDowell, Fay Kanin and Richard Brooks.

of humiliations that were intended to teach her to keep her place and be grateful for it. But she saw that there were rules to the game, if one were talented enough and bold enough to use them. If her bosses showed her few courtesies, she in turn showed them little mercy when she reached the point where acting talent could be converted into worldly power. Attack became her preferred means of defence; and it formed her stardom accordingly.

No other film actress of her era had such a capacity for acting in ways that attracted and yet unsettled (often at one and the same time) the leading men in her movies. Her extraordinary physical features befitted her uniquely for this. Those eyes will fortunately be better preserved in film history than any medical formaldehyde could manage. If looks could kill, then Davis would, willy nilly, have been a Lady Macbeth who did not need her murder-bent mate to hand his daggers over to her – her eyes were *her* daggers. That voice, too! Equipped with such a regal silencer, she learned to modu-

late its tones to fit the whole range of roles known to humanity (and some known only to screenwriters). In tearjerkers like *Now, Voyager* and *Dark Victory*, it could become a universal solvent to soften up an audience; in *The Letter* and *The Little Foxes*, an annealing agent to harden the same admirers against her implacable villainess. And in *All About Eve*, she showed how she could subsume her mannered looks and locutions into the most humanly rounded role she ever played, so that her *prima donna* took on the aspect of Everywoman.

Such an actress simply could not help provoking a reaction in millions of men and women. But her influence was probably strongest on the latter. She offered women a role model, long before that term slipped into common use (and over-use). Her example showed them how to claw their way to power and also how to cast away selfish advantage; how to nourish murder in the heart and also hold self-sacrifice in reserve in their soul; how to stay in charge of a man and also how to yield

174

posite, With James
wart in the American
film *Right of Way*.

mily reunion' right: as
ew England teacher
the verge of retirement
a 1984 TV special,
te discovers that one
her ex-students in the
vie is played by real-
grandson Ashley
man.

face and figure are
ner from a recent
ration, (far right) but
step is as firm as ever.
th secretary and
urity man in tow and
Agatha Christie film
ind her, Bette Davis
ves London Airport by
ncorde at the end of
4 in search of new
es: *'Untold want, by
and land 'nere
nted,/ Now, Voyager,
thou forth to seek and
' – Whitman.*

to him (for the time being) with good and loving grace.

She gave women a taste of power other than in terms of sexual power. It may well be that her most loyal admirers were those attracted by the examples she provided for acquisitive womanhood in a country where a disproportionate amount of wealth was coming into the hands of a sex who were disenfranchised for much of the time from imposing themselves on society in other ways. Davis's stardom matched the graph of the control that American women exercised over areas of the nation's life and economy in wartime – and it subsided as women retreated (or were pushed back) into their 'traditional' roles in the home and family, two institutions that some of Davis's most popular roles, like *Jezebel*, had revealed as restricting a woman's instinct for independence. She set the example by rebelling; and even if circumstances deterred most women from emulating her, they followed her thrilling wilfulness vicariously through her performances.

There is a strong link between Bette Davis and Elizabeth Taylor, in more than simply the fact that both of them played the same role in film and stage versions of *The Little Foxes*. Taylor was also an actress who was able to impose herself, at the height of her stardom or, as some would say, her notoriety, on a Hollywood that had also done her much psychic damage in her time and on a mass public fascinated by her defiance of convention. Both actresses also had a fondness for playing roles in which cash was frequently the nexus of the heroine's emotions. Both of them seemed the sum of lengthy careers that had known ups and downs, but authenticated their existence in ways denied to many modern nobodies whose images are pitifully dependent on the run of their mini-series. Neither Davis nor Taylor was a 'come and go' creation: they were stayers. Of course, compared with the 'indecent exposure' that Taylor's public and private life invited or suffered, Davis looks like a recluse. This is where they differ. Davis's life was immured in her work: Taylor's work was dissipated in her life. Yet both women have stayed stars far beyond the natural term of such a phenomenon by their ability to *impose* themselves on art and life in ways that flagrantly neglect the rules and bring them penalties that have sometimes been costly and painful. 'My joy in working was never just playing the heroine,' Davis has claimed. Where Taylor excelled, she too broke with conventional expectations. Taylor has not (yet) done so as luridly as Davis in her gothic shocker *What Ever Happened to Baby Jane?* although her own *Who's Afraid of Virginia Woolf?* echoes its domestic argy-bargy as well as its teasing note of interrogation. But both stars gave the impression that they didn't give a damn what they did, or what was thought about them, so long as it provided fun and a fee – and, in Davis's case, professional risk.

Davis, finally, demonstrated to women that sex appeal could be connoted by sheer will-power. For a long time, Warner Bros couldn't see it that way. But women could – and did. The film critic who reported on Davis's performance in *Of Human Bondage* said euphemistically that she was 'effective in pathological mazes which the cinema rarely dares to examine.' What he was getting at – for, of course, it was a 'he' – was her perverse nature, her bitchiness. But her own sex did not view her art in such a narrow way. They judged her for the way she represented the will to action on screen, and off, for six decades; and they found her good.

ACKNOWLEDGEMENTS

The author wishes to acknowledge his indebtedness to the authors and editors of the following works quoted from or referred to in the text:

Charles Affron, *Star Acting* (E. P. Dutton, New York: 1977)
Mary Astor, *A Life on Film* (Delacorte Press, New York: 1971)
John Baxter, *Hollywood in the Thirties* (Zwemmer, London; Barnes, New York: 1968)
Bette Davis, *The Lonely Life* (G. P. Puttnam's Sons, New York: 1962)
Gordon Gow, *Hollywood in the Fifties* (Zwemmer, London; Barnes, New York: 1971)
Graham Greene, *The Pleasure Dome*, ed. John Russell Taylor (Secker and Warburg, London: 1972)
Charles Higham, *Bette* (Macmillan, New York: 1981)
Charles Higham and Joel Greenberg, *The Celluloid Muse* (Angus and Robertson, London: 1969)
Charles Higham and Joel Greenberg, *Hollywood in the Forties* (Zwemmer, London; Barnes, New York: 1968)
Joseph L. Mankiewicz and Gary Carey, *More About All About Eve* (Random House, New York: 1972)
Danny Peary, *Close-Ups* (Workman Publishing, New York: 1978)
Rex Reed, *Conversations in the Raw* (New American Library, New York: 1969)
Gene Ringgold, *The Films of Bette Davis* (Citadel Press Secaucus, New Jersey: 1966; updated by Lawrence J. Quirk, 1985)
Nick Roddick, *A New Deal in Entertainment: Warner Brothers in the 1930s* (British Film Institute, London: 1983)
Marjorie Rosen, *Popcorn Venus* (Peter Owen, London: 1973)
Richard Schickel, *The Stars* (Bonanza Books, New York: 1962)
David O. Selznick, *A Memo from David O. Selznick*, ed. Rudy Behlmer (Macmillan, London: 1973)
Whitney Stine, *Mother Goddam* with a commentary by Bette Davis (W. H. Allen, London: 1974)
Parker Tyler, *Magic and Myth of the Movies* (Secker and Warburg, London: 1971)
Frank Westmore and Muriel Davidson, *The Westmores of Hollywood* (W. H. Allen, London: 1976)

Quotations from various film critics of *The New York Times* derive from the collected edition of *New York Times Film Reviews* published by the Arno Press, New York.

Quotations are acknowledged from the following periodicals: *Film Weekly, Focus on Film, Modern Screen, Photoplay, Picture Post, The Spectator, Sight and Sound.*

The author's interviews with Miss Davis, portions of which form the preface to this book, originally appeared in the London *Evening Standard*, 29 June 1967, and the March 1978 and March 1985 issues of British *Vogue*. They are reproduced here by kind permission, respectively, of Louis Kirby, editor of *The London Standard*, and Esco Ltd, and Beatrix Miller, editor-in-chief of British *Vogue* and Condé Nast Publications Ltd. For assistance in viewing many of the Bette Davis films, I owe a particularly warm debt to the facilities offered me by Jack and Elizabeth Lodge and Peter Seward.

FILMOGRAPHY

1 Bad Sister △
DIRECTOR Hobart Henley
SCENARIO Raymond L Schrock and Tom Reed, with additional dialogue by Edwin Knopf, based on the novel *The Flirt* by Booth Tarkington
PHOTOGRAPHY Karl Freund
EDITOR Ted Kent
CAST Conrad Nagel, Sidney Fox, Bette Davis, Zasu Pitts, Slim Summerville, Charles Winninger, Emma Dunn, Humphrey Bogart, Bert Roach, David Durand
RUNNING TIME 68 minutes
RELEASED 29 March 1931
PRODUCED BY Universal Pictures

2 Seed △
DIRECTOR John M Stahl
SCENARIO Gladys Lehman, based on the novel of the same name by Charles G Norris
PHOTOGRAPHY Jackson Rose
EDITOR Arthur Taveres

CAST John Boles, Genevieve Tobin, Lois Wilson, Raymond Hackett, Bette Davis, Frances Dade, Zasu Pitts, Richard Tucker, Jack Willis, Don Cox, Dick Winslow, Kenneth Selling, Terry Cox, Helen Parrish, Dickie Moore
RUNNING TIME 96 minutes
RELEASED 14 May 1931
PRODUCED BY Universal Pictures

3 Waterloo Bridge △
DIRECTOR James Whale
SCENARIO Benn W Levy, with continuity and additional dialogue by Tom Reed, based on the play of the same name by Robert E Sherwood
PHOTOGRAPHY Arthur Edeson
EDITOR James Whale
CAST Mae Clarke, Kent Douglas (Douglass Montgomery), Doris Lloyd, Ethel Griffies, Enid Bennett, Frederick Kerr, Bette Davis, Rita Carlisle
RUNNING TIME 72 minutes
RELEASED 4 September 1931
PRODUCED BY Universal Pictures

4 Way Back Home ▽
DIRECTOR William A Seiter
SCENARIO *Other People's Business* by Jane

Murfin, based on radio characters created by Phillips Lord
PHOTOGRAPHY J Roy Hunt
CAST Phillips Lord, Effie Palmer, Mrs Phillips Lord, Bennett Kilpack, Raymond Hunter, Frank Albertson, Bette Davis, Oscar Apfel, Stanley Fields, Dorothy Peterson, Frankie Darro
RUNNING TIME 81 minutes
RELEASED 15 January 1932
PRODUCED BY RKO Radio

5 The Menace △
DIRECTOR Roy William Neill
SCENARIO Dorothy Howell and Charles Logue, with additional dialogue by Roy Chanslor, based on the novel *The Feathered Serpent* by Edgar Wallace
PHOTOGRAPHY L William O'Connell
EDITOR Gene Havelick
CAST H B Warner, Bette Davis, Walter Byron, Natalie Moorhead, William B Davidson, Crauford Kent, Halliwell Hobbes, Charles Gerrard, Murray Kinnell
RUNNING TIME 64 minutes
RELEASED 29 January 1932
PRODUCED BY Colombia

6 Hell's House ▷
DIRECTOR Howard Higgins
SCENARIO Paul Gangelin and B Harrison Orkow, based on a story by Howard Higgins
PHOTOGRAPHY Allen S Siegel
EDITOR Edward Schroeder
CAST Junior Durkin, Pat O'Brien, Bette Davis, Junior Coughlan, Charley Grapewin, Emma Dunn, James Marcus, Morgan Wallace, Wallis Clark, Hooper Atchley

RUNNING TIME 72 minutes
RELEASED 30 January 1932
PRODUCED BY Capitol Films

RUNNING TIME 82 minutes
RELEASED 29 April 1932
PRODUCED BY Warner Brothers Vitaphone

Melville Crossman, Joseph Jackson and
Courtenay Terrett
PHOTOGRAPHY Sol Polito
EDITOR George Marks
CAST Warren William, Bette Davis, Guy
Kibbee, Frank McHugh, Vivienne Osborne,
Sam Hardy, Robert Warwick, Harry
Holman, Charles Sellon, Robert Emmett
O'Connor, Berton Churchill
RUNNING TIME 75 minutes
RELEASED 8 June 1932
PRODUCED BY First National Pictures,
released by Warner Bros

11 Cabin In The Cotton △
DIRECTOR Michael Curtiz
SCENARIO Paul Green, based on the novel of
the same name by Harry Harrison Kroll
PHOTOGRAPHY Barney McGill
EDITOR George Amy
CAST Richard Barthelmess, Bette Davis,
Dorothy Jordan, Henry B Walthall, Berton
Churchill, Walter Percival, William L
Maired, Hardie Albright, Edmund Breese,
Tully Marshall, Clarence Muse, Russell
Simpson, John Marston, Erville Anderson,
Dorothy Peterson, Snow Flake, Harry
Cording
RUNNING TIME 79 minutes
RELEASED 29 September 1932
PRODUCED BY First National Pictures,
released by Warner Bros

7 The Man Who Played God △
DIRECTOR John Adolfi
SCENARIO Julien Josephson and Maude T
Howell, adapted from a short story by
Gouverneur Morris and the play *The Silent
Voice* by Jules Eckert Goodman
PHOTOGRAPHY James Van Trees
EDITOR William Holmes
CAST George Arliss, Violet Heming, Ivan
Simpson, Louise Closser Hale, Bette Davis,
Donald Cook, Paul Porcasi, Oscar Apfel,
William Janney, Grace Durkin, Dorothy
Libaire, Andre Luget, Charles Evans,
Murray Kinnell, Wade Boteler, Alexander
Ikonikoff
RUNNING TIME 80 minutes
RELEASED 10 February 1932
PRODUCED BY Warner Brothers Vitaphone

8 So Big ▽
DIRECTOR William A Wellman
SCENARIO J Grubb Alexander and Robert
Lord, based on the novel of the same name
by Edna Ferber
PHOTOGRAPHY Sid Hickox
EDITOR William Holmes
CAST Barbara Stanwyck, George Brent,
Dickie Moore, Bette Davis, Guy Kibee,
Mae Madison, Hardie Albright, Robert
Warwick, Arthur Stone, Earl Foxe, Alan
Hale, Dorothy Peterson, Dawn O'Day
(Anne Shirley), Dick Winslow, Elizabeth
Patterson, Rita LeRoy, Blanche Friderici,
Lionel Bellmore

9 The Rich Are Always With Us △
DIRECTOR Alfred E Green
SCENARIO Austin Parker, based on the novel
of the same name by E Pettit
PHOTOGRAPHY Ernest Haller
EDITOR George Marks
CAST Ruth Chatterton, George Brent,
Adrienne Dore, Bette Davis, John Miljan,
Mae Madison, John Wray, Robert
Warwick, Virginia Hammond, Walter
Walker, Eula Gray, Edith Allen, Ethel
Kenyon, Ruth Lee, Berton Churchill
RUNNING TIME 73 minutes
RELEASED 15 May 1932
PRODUCED BY First National Pictures,
released by Warner Bros

10 The Dark Horse ▽
DIRECTOR Alfred E Green
SCENARIO Joseph Jackson and Wilson
Mizner, based on an original story by

12 Three on a Match △
DIRECTOR Mervyn LeRoy
SCENARIO Lucien Hubbard, based on an
original story by Kubec Glasmon and John
Bright
PHOTOGRAPHY Sol Polito
EDITOR Ray Curtiss
CAST Joan Blondell, Warren William, Ann
Dvorak, Bette Davis, Grant Mitchell, Lyle
Talbot, Sheila Terry, Glenda Farrell, Clara
Blandick, Buster Phelps, Humphrey Bogart,

John Marston, Patricia Ellis, Hale Hamilton, Frankie Darro, Dawn O'Day, (Anne Shirley), Virginia Davis, Dick Brandon, Allen Jenkins, Jack LaRue, Edward Arnold
RUNNING TIME 63 minutes
RELEASED 28 October 1932
PRODUCED BY First National Pictures, released by Warner Bros

13 20,000 Years In Sing Sing △
DIRECTOR Michael Curtiz
SCENARIO Wilson Mizner and Brown Holmes, adaptation by Courtenay Terrett and Robert Lord, based on the book of the same name by Warden Lewis E Lawes
PHOTOGRAPHY Barney McGill
EDITOR George Amy
CAST Spencer Tracy, Bette Davis, Lyle Talbot, Arthur Byron, Sheila Terry, Edward McNamara, Warren Hymer, Louis Calhern, Spencer Charters, Sam Godfrey, Grant Mitchell, Nella Walker, Harold Huber, William Le Maire, Arthur Hoyt, George Pat Collins
RUNNING TIME 77 minutes
RELEASED 9 January 1933
PRODUCED BY First National Pictures, released by Warner Bros

14 Parachute Jumper △
DIRECTOR Alfred E Green
SCENARIO John Francis Larkin, based on the story *Some Call It Love* by Rian James
PHOTOGRAPHY James Van Trees
EDITOR Ray Curtiss
CAST Douglas Fairbanks Jr, Leo Carrillo, Bette Davis, Frank McHugh, Claire Dodd, Sheila Terry, Harold Huber, Thomas E Jackson, George Pat Collins, Pat O'Malley, Harold Healy, Ferdinand Munley, Walter Miller
RUNNING TIME 65 minutes
RELEASED 25 January 1933
PRODUCED BY Warner Bros

15 The Working Man △
DIRECTOR John Adolfi
SCENARIO Maude T Howell and Charles Kenyon, based on the story *The Adopted Father* by Edgar Franklin
PHOTOGRAPHY Sol Polito
EDITOR Owen Marks
CAST George Arliss, Bette Davis, Hardie Albright, Theodore Newton, Gordon Westcott, J Farrell MacDonald, Charles Evans, Frederick Burton, Edward Van Sloan, Pat Wing, Claire McDowell, Harold Minjir, Douglas Dumbrille
RUNNING TIME 73 minutes
RELEASED 20 April 1933
PRODUCED BY Warner Bros Vitaphone

16 Ex-Lady △
DIRECTOR Robert Florey
SCENARIO David Boehm, based on an original story by Edith Fitzgerald and Robert Riskin
PHOTOGRAPHY Tony Gaudio
EDITOR Harold McLernon
CAST Bette Davis, Gene Raymond, Frank McHugh, Monroe Owsley, Claire Dodd, Kay Strozzi, Ferdinand Gottschalk, Alphonse Ethier, Bodil Rosing
RUNNING TIME 62 minutes
RELEASED 14 May 1933
PRODUCED BY Warner Bros Vitaphone

17 Bureau of Missing Persons ▽
DIRECTOR Roy Del Ruth
SCENARIO Robert Presnell, based on the book *Missing Men* by Police Captain John H Ayers and Carol Bird

PHOTOGRAPHY Barney McGill
EDITOR James Gibbon
CAST Bette Davis, Lewis Stone, Pat O'Brien, Glenda Farrell, Allen Jenkins, Ruth Donnelly, Hugh Herbert, Alan Dinehart, Marjorie Gateson, Tad Alexander, Noel Francis, Wallis Clark, Adrian Morris, Clay Clement, Henry Kolker, Harry Beresford, George Chandler
RUNNING TIME 75 minutes
RELEASED 8 September 1933
PRODUCED BY First National Pictures, released by Warner Bros

18 Fashions Of 1934 △
DIRECTOR William Dieterle
SCENARIO F Hugh Herbert, Gene Markey, Kathryn Scola and Carl Erickson, based on the story *The Fashion Place* by Harry Collins and Warren Duff
PHOTOGRAPHY William Rees
EDITOR Jack Killifer
CAST William Powell, Bette Davis, Frank McHugh, Verree Teasdale, Reginald Owen, Henry O'Neill, Philip Reed, Hugh Herbert, Gordon Westcott, Nella Walker, Dorothy Burgess, Etienne Girardot, William Burress, Spencer Charters, Jane Darwell, Arthur Treacher, Hobart Cavanaugh, Albert Conti
RUNNING TIME 77 minutes
RELEASED 19 January 1934
PRODUCED BY First National Pictures, released by Warner Bros

19 The Big Shakedown ▷
DIRECTOR John Francis Dillon
SCENARIO Niven Busch and Rian James, based on the story *Cut Rate* by Samuel Engel
PHOTOGRAPHY Sid Hickox
EDITOR James Gibbons
CAST Charles Farrell, Bette Davis, Ricardo Cortez, Glenda Farrell, Allen Jenkins, Henry O'Neill, Philip Faversham, Robert Emmett O'Connor, John Wray, George Pat

Collins, Adrian Morris, Dewey Robinson, Samuel S Hinds, Matt Briggs, William B Davison, Earl Foxe, Frederick Burton
RUNNING TIME 64 minutes
RELEASED 11 February 1934
PRODUCED BY First National Pictures, released by Warner Bros

20 Jimmy The Gent △
DIRECTOR Michael Curtiz
SCENARIO Bertram Milhauser, based on the story *The Heir Chaser* by Laird Doyle and Ray Nazarro
PHOTOGRAPHY Ira Morgan
EDITOR Tommy Richards
CAST James Cagney, Bette Davis, Alice White, Allen Jenkins, Arthur Hohl, Alan Dinehart, Philip Reed, Hobart Cavanaugh, Mayo Methot, Ralf Harolde, Joseph Sawyer, Philip Faversham, Nora Lane, Howard Hickman, Jane Darwell, Joseph Crehan, Robert Warwick, Harold Entwhistle
RUNNING TIME 66 minutes
RELEASED 25 March 1934
PRODUCED BY Warner Bros Vitaphone

21 Fog Over Frisco ▽
DIRECTOR William Dieterle
SCENARIO Robert N Lee and Eugene Solow,

based on an original story by George Dyer, *The Five Fragments*
PHOTOGRAPHY Tony Gaudio
EDITOR Harold McLernon
CAST Bette Davis, Donald Woods, Margaret Lindsay, Lyle Talbot, Arthur Byron, Hugh Herbert, Douglas Dumbrille, Robert Barrat, Henry O'Neill, Irving Pichel, Gordon Westcott, Charles C Wilson, Allen Hale, William B Davidson, Douglas Cosgrove, George Chandler, Harold Minjir, William Demarest
RUNNING TIME 67 minutes
RELEASED 6 June 1934
PRODUCED BY Warner Bros Vitaphone

22 Of Human Bondage △
DIRECTOR John Cromwell
SCENARIO Lester Cohen, based on the novel of the same name by W Somerset Maugham
PHOTOGRAPHY Henry W Gerrard
EDITOR William Morgan
CAST Leslie Howard, Bette Davis, Frances Dee, Kay Johnson, Reginald Denny, Alan Hale, Reginald Owen, Reginald Sheffield, Desmond Roberts
RUNNING TIME 83 minutes
RELEASED 28 June 1934
PRODUCED BY RKO Radio

23 Housewife △
DIRECTOR Alfred E Green
SCENARIO Manuel Seff and Lillie Hayward, based on an original story by Robert Lord and Lillie Hayward
PHOTOGRAPHY William Rees
EDITOR James Gibbon

CAST George Brent, Bette Davis, Ann Dvorak, John Halliday, Ruth Donnelly, Hobart Cavanaugh, Robert Barrat, Joseph Cawthorn, Phil Regan, Willard Robertson, Ronald Cosbey, Leila Bennett, William B Davidson, John Hale
RUNNING TIME 69 minutes
RELEASED 9 August 1934
PRODUCED BY Warner Bros Vitaphone

24 Bordertown △
DIRECTOR Archie Mayo
SCENARIO Laird Doyle and Wallace Smith, adapted by Robert Lord, based on the novel of the same name by Carroll Graham
PHOTOGRAPHY Tony Gaudio
EDITOR Thomas Richards
CAST Paul Muni, Bette Davis, Margaret Lindsay, Gavin Gordon, Arthur Stone, Robert Barrat, Soledad Jiminez, Eugene Pallette, William B Davidson, Hobart Cavanaugh, Henry O'Neill, Vivian Tobin, Nella Walker, Oscar Apfel, Samuel S Hinds, Chris Pin Martin, Frank Puglia, Jack Norton
RUNNING TIME 80 minutes
RELEASED 23 January 1935
PRODUCED BY Warner Bros Vitaphone

25 The Girl From Tenth Avenue △
DIRECTOR Alfred E Green
SCENARIO Charles Kenyon, based on a play by Hubert Henry Davies
PHOTOGRAPHY James Van Trees
EDITOR Owen Marks
CAST Bette Davis, Ian Hunter, Colin Clive, Alison Skipworth, John Eldredge, Philip Reed, Katherine Alexander, Helen Jerome Eddy, Gordon Elliott, Adrian Rosley,

Andre Cheron, Edward McWade, Mary
Treen, Heinie Conklin
RUNNING TIME 69 minutes
RELEASED 26 May 1935
PRODUCED BY First National Pictures,
released by Warner Bros

26 Front Page Woman △
DIRECTOR Michael Curtiz
SCENARIO Roy Chanslor, Lillie Hayward
and Laird Doyle, based on the story *Women
Are Bum Newspapermen* by Richard
Macaulay
PHOTOGRAPHY Tony Gaudio
EDITOR Terry Morse
CAST Bette Davis, George Brent, June
Martel, Dorothy Dare, Joseph Crehan,
Winifred Shaw, Roscoe Karns, Joseph
King, J Farrell MacDonald, J Carroll
Naish, Walter Walker, DeWitt Jennings,
Huntley Gordon, Adrian Rosley, Georges
Renevent, Grace Hale, Selmer Jackson,
Gordon Westcott
RUNNING TIME 80 minutes
RELEASED 11 July 1935
PRODUCED BY Warner Bros Vitaphone

27 Special Agent △
DIRECTOR William Keighley
SCENARIO Laird Doyle and Abem Finkel,
based on an idea by Martin Mooney
PHOTOGRAPHY Sid Hickox
EDITOR Clarence Kouster
CAST Bette Davis, George Brent, Ricardo
Cortez, Jack LaRue, Henry O'Neill, Robert
Strange, Joseph Crehan, J Carroll Naish,
Joseph Sawyer, William B Davidson,
Robert Barrat, Paul Guilfoyle, Irving
Pichel, Douglas Wood, James Flavin, Lee
Phelps, Louis Natheaux, Herbert Skinner,
John Alexander
RUNNING TIME 76 minutes
RELEASED 18 September 1935
PRODUCED BY Claridge Pictures, released by
Warner Bros

28 Dangerous △
DIRECTOR Alfred E Green
SCENARIO and original by Laird Doyle
PHOTOGRAPHY Ernest Haller
CAST Bette Davis, Franchot Tone, Margaret
Lindsay, Alison Skipworth, John Eldredge,
Dick Foran, Walter Walker, Richard Carle,
George Irving, Pierre Watkin, Douglas
Wood, William B Davidson, Frank
O'Connor, Edward Keane
RUNNING TIME 78 minutes
RELEASED 25 December 1935
PRODUCED BY Warner Bros Vitaphone

29 The Petrified Forest △
DIRECTOR Archie Mayo
SCENARIO Charles Kenyon and Delmer
Daves, based on the play of the same name
by Robert E Sherwood
PHOTOGRAPHY Sol Polito
EDITOR Owen Marks
CAST Leslie Howard, Bette Davis,
Genevieve Tobin, Dick Foran, Humphrey
Bogart, Joseph Sawyer, Porter Hall,
Charley Grapewin, Paul Harvey, Eddie
Acuff, Adrian Morris, Nina Campana, Slim
Johnson, John Alexander
RUNNING TIME 75 minutes
RELEASED 6 February 1936
PRODUCED BY Warner Bros Vitaphone

30 The Golden Arrow ▽
DIRECTOR Alfred E Green
SCENARIO Charles Kenyon, based on the
play *Dream Princess* by Michael Arlen
PHOTOGRAPHY Arthur Edeson
EDITOR Thomas Pratt
CAST Bette Davis, George Brent, Eugene

Pallette, Dick Foran, Carol Hughes,
Catherine Doucet, Craig Reynolds, Ivan
Lebedeff, G P Huntley Jr, Hobart
Cavanaugh, Henry O'Neill, Eddie Acuff,
Earl Foxe, E E Clive, Rafael Storm, Sara
Edwards, Bess Flowers, Mary Treen,
Selmer Jackson
RUNNING TIME 68 minutes
RELEASED 3 May 1936
PRODUCED BY First National Pictures,
released by Warner Bros

31 Satan Met A Lady △
DIRECTOR William Dieterle
SCENARIO Brown Holmes, based on the
novel *The Maltese Falcon* by Dashiell
Hammett
PHOTOGRAPHY Arthur Edeson
EDITOR Max Parker, re-edited by Warren
Low
CAST Bette Davis, Warren William, Alison
Skipworth, Arthur Treacher, Winifred
Shaw, Marie Wilson, Porter Hall, Maynard
Holmes, Olin Howard, Charles Wilson,
Joseph King, Barbara Blane, William B
Davidson
RUNNING TIME 66 minutes
RELEASED 22 July 1936
PRODUCED BY Warner Bros Vitaphone

32 Marked Woman △
DIRECTOR Lloyd Bacon
SCENARIO Robert Rosson and Abem Finkel,
with additional dialogue by Seton I Miller
PHOTOGRAPHY George Barnes
EDITOR Jack Killifer

CAST Bette Davis, Humphrey Bogart, Eduardo Ciannelli, Jane Bryan, Lola Lane, Isabel Jewell, Rosalind Marquis, Mayo Methot, Ben Welden, Henry O'Neill, Allen Jenkins, John Litel, Damian O'Flynn, Robert Strange, Raymond Hatton, William B Davidson, Frank Faylen, Jack Norton, Kenneth Harlan
RUNNING TIME 96 minutes
RELEASED 11 April 1937
PRODUCED BY Warner Bros, First National Pictures

33 Kid Galahad △
DIRECTOR Michael Curtiz
SCENARIO Seton I Miller, based on the novel of the same name by Francis Wallace
PHOTOGRAPHY Tony Gaudio
EDITOR George Amy
CAST Edward G Robinson, Bette Davis, Humphrey Bogart, Wayne Morris, William Haade, Jane Bryan, Harry Carey, Soledad Jiminez, Veda Ann Borg, Ben Welden, Joseph Crehan, Harlan Tucker, Frank Faylen, Joyce Compton, Horace MacMahon
RUNNING TIME 100 minutes
RELEASED 26 May 1937
PRODUCED BY Warner Bros

34 That Certain Woman △
DIRECTOR Edmund Goulding
SCENARIO Edmund Goulding, based on his original screenplay, *The Trespasser*
PHOTOGRAPHY Ernest Haller
EDITOR Jack Killifer
CAST Bette Davis, Henry Fonda, Ian Hunter, Anita Louise, Donald Crisp, Katherine Alexander, Mary Phillips, Minor Watson, Ben Welden, Sidney Toler, Charles Trowbridge, Norman Willis, Herbert Rawlinson, Rosalind Marquis, Frank Faylen, Willard Parker, Dwane Day, Hugh O'Connell

RUNNING TIME 91 minutes
RELEASED 15 September 1937
PRODUCED BY Warner Bros, First National Pictures

35 Its Love I'm After △
DIRECTOR Archie Mayo
SCENARIO Casey Robinson, based on the story *Gentlemen After Midnight* by Maurice Hanline
PHOTOGRAPHY James Van Trees
EDITOR Owen Marks
CAST Leslie Howard, Bette Davis, Olivia De Havilland, Patric Knowles, Eric Blore, George Barbier, Spring Byington, Bonita Granville, E E Clive, Veda Ann Borg, Valerie Bergere, Georgia Caine, Sarah Edwards, Lionel Bellmore, Irving Bacon
RUNNING TIME 90 minutes
RELEASED 10 November 1937
PRODUCED BY Warner Bros

36 Jezebel △
DIRECTOR William Wyler
SCENARIO Clements Ripley, Abem Finkel and John Huston, with the help of Robert Buckner, based on the play of the same name by Owen Davis Sr
PHOTOGRAPHY Ernest Haller
EDITOR Warren Low
CAST Bette Davis, Henry Fonda, George Brent, Donald Crisp, Fay Bainter, Margaret Lindsay, Henry O'Neill, John Litel, Gordon Oliver, Spring Byington, Margaret Early, Richard Cromwell, Theresa Harris, Janet Shaw, Irving Pichel, Eddie Anderson
RUNNING TIME 100 minutes
RELEASED 10 March 1938
PRODUCED BY Warner Bros

37 The Sisters ▽
DIRECTOR Anatole Litvak
SCENARIO Milton Krims, based on the novel of the same name by Myron Brinig
PHOTOGRAPHY Tony Gaudio
EDITOR Warren Low

CAST Errol Flynn, Bette Davis, Anita Louise, Ian Hunter, Donald Crisp, Beulah Bondi, Jane Bryan, Alan Hale, Dick Foran, Henry Travers, Patric Knowles, Lee Patrick, Laura Hope Crewes, Janet Shaw, Harry Davenport, Ruth Garland, John Warburton, Paul Harvey, Mayo Methot, Irving Bacon, Arthur Hoyt
RUNNING TIME 95 minutes
RELEASED 14 October 1938
PRODUCED BY Warner Bros

38 Dark Victory △
DIRECTOR Edmund Goulding
SCENARIO Casey Robinson, based on the play of the same name by George Emerson Brewer Jr and Bertram Block
PHOTOGRAPHY Ernest Haller
EDITOR William Holmes
CAST Bette Davis, George Brent, Geraldine Fitzgerald, Humphrey Bogart, Ronald Reagan, Henry Travers, Cora Witherspoon, Dorothy Peterson, Virginia Brissac, Charles Richman, Leonard Mudie, Fay Helm, Lottie Williams
RUNNING TIME 105 minutes
RELEASED 20 April 1939
PRODUCED BY Warner Bros, First National Pictures

39 Juarez ▽
DIRECTOR William Dieterle
SCENARIO John Huston, Aeneas MacKenzie and Wolfgang Reinhardt, based on the play *Juarez and Maximilian* by Franz Werfel and the book *The Phantom Crown* by Bertita Harding
PHOTOGRAPHY Tony Gaudio
EDITOR Warren Low
CAST Paul Muni, Bette Davis, Brian Aherne, Claude Rains, John Garfield, Donald Crisp, Joseph Calleia, Gale Sondergaard, Gilbert Roland, Henry O'Neill, Harry Davenport, Louis Calhern, Walter Kingsford, Georgia Caine, Montagu Love, John Miljan,

Vladmir Sokoloff, Irving Pichel, Pedro De Cordoba, Gilbert Emory, Monte Blue, Manuel Diaz, Hugh Sothern, Mickey Kuhn
RUNNING TIME 125 minutes
RELEASED 25 April 1939
PRODUCED BY Warner Bros

40 The Old Maid △
DIRECTOR Edmund Goulding
SCENARIO Casey Robinson, based on the Pulitzer Prize play by Zoe Atkins, adapted from the novel of the same name by Edith Wharton
PHOTOGRAPHY Tony Gaudio
EDITOR George Amy
CAST Bette Davis, Miriam Hopkins, George Brent, Donald Crisp, Jane Bryan, Louise Fazenda, James Stephenson, Jerome Cowan, William Lundigan, Rand Brooks, Cecelia Loftus, Janet Shaw, DeWolf Hopper
RUNNING TIME 95 minutes
RELEASED 11 August 1939
PRODUCED BY Warner Bros, First National Pictures

41 The Private Lives Of Elizabeth And Essex ▽
DIRECTOR Michael Curtiz
SCENARIO Norman Reilly Raine and Aeneas MacKenzie, based on the play *Elizabeth the Queen* by Maxwell Anderson
PHOTOGRAPHY Sol Polito and H Howard Greene
EDITOR Owen Marks

CAST Bette Davis, Errol Flynn, Olivia de Havilland, Donald Crisp, Vincent Price, Alan Hale, Henry Stephenson, Henry Daniell, James Stephenson, Leo G Carroll, Nanette Fabares (Fabray), Rosella Towne, Maris Wrixon, Ralph Forbes, Robert Warwick, John Sutton, Guy Bellis, Doris Lloyd, Forrester Harvey
RUNNING TIME 105 minutes
RELEASED 1 December 1939
PRODUCED BY Warner Bros

42 All This And Heaven Too △
DIRECTOR Anatole Litvak
SCENARIO Casey Robinson, based on the novel of the same name by Rachel Field
PHOTOGRAPHY Ernest Haller
EDITOR Warren Low
CAST Bette Davis, Charles Boyer, Jeffrey Lynn, Barbara O'Neill, Virginia Weidler, Helen Westley, Walter Hampden, Henry Daniell, Harry Davenport, George Coulouris, Montague Love, Janet Beecher, June Lockhart, Ann Todd, Richard Nichols, Fritz Leiber, Ian Keith, Sibyl Harris, Mary Anderson, Edward Fielding, Ann Gillis, Peggy Stewart, Victor Kilian, Mrs Gardner Crane
RUNNING TIME 105 minutes
RELEASED 4 July 1940
PRODUCED BY Warner Bros, First National Pictures

43 The Letter ▽
DIRECTOR William Wyler
SCENARIO Howard Koch, based on the play of the same name by W Somerset Maugham
PHOTOGRAPHY Tony Gaudio
EDITOR George Amy
CAST Bette Davis, Herbert Marshall, James Stephenson, Frieda Inescort, Gale Sondergaard, Bruce Lester (David Bruce), Elizabeth Earl, Cecil Kellaway, Doris Lloyd, Sen Yung, Willie Fung, Tetsu Komai, Roland Got, Otto Hahn, Pete

Kotehernaro, David Newell, Ottola Nesmith, Lilian Kemble-Cooper
RUNNING TIME 95 minutes
RELEASED 22 November 1940
PRODUCED BY Warner Bros, First National Pictures

44 The Great Lie △
DIRECTOR Edmund Goulding
SCENARIO Lenore Coffee, based on the novel *January Heights* by Polan Banks
PHOTOGRAPHY Tony Gaudio
EDITOR Ralph Dawson
CAST Bette Davis, George Brent, Mary Aston, Lucile Watson, Hattie McDaniel, Grant Mitchell, Jerome Cowan, Sam McDaniel, Thurston Hall, Russell Hicks, Charles Trowbridge, Virginia Brissac, Olin Howland, J Farrell MacDonald, Doris Lloyd, Addison Richards, Georgia Caine, Alphonse Martell
RUNNING TIME 102 minutes
RELEASED 11 April 1941
PRODUCED BY Warner Bros

45 The Bride Came C.O.D. ▽
DIRECTOR William Keighley
SCENARIO Julius J and Philip G Epstein, based on a story by Kenneth Earl and M M Musselman
PHOTOGRAPHY Ernest Haller
EDITOR Thomas Richards
CAST James Cagney, Bette Davis, Stuart Erwin, Jack Carson, George Tobias, Eugene Pallette, Harry Davenport, William Frawley, Edward Brophy, Harry Holman, Chick Chandler, Keith Douglas, Herbert Anderson, Creighton Hale, Frank Mayo,

DeWolf Hopper, Jack Mower, William Newell
RUNNING TIME 90 minutes
RELEASED 25 July 1941
PRODUCED BY Warner Bros

46 The Little Foxes △
DIRECTOR William Wyler
SCENARIO Lilian Hellman, based on her stage play of the same name, with additional scenes and dialogue by Arthur Kober, Dorothy Parker and Alan Campbell
PHOTOGRAPHY Gregg Toland
EDITOR Daniel Mandell
CAST Bette Davis, Herbert Marshall, Teresa Wright, Richard Carlson, Patricia Collinge, Dan Duryea, Charles Dingle, Carl Benton Reid, Jessie Grayson, John Marriott, Russell Hicks, Lucien Littlefield, Virginia Brissac
RUNNING TIME 115 minutes
RELEASED 21 August 1941
PRODUCED BY Samuel Goldwyn Productions, released by RKO Radio

47 The Man Who Came To Dinner ▽
DIRECTOR William Keighley
SCENARIO Julius J and Philip G Epstein, based on the play of the same name by

George S Kaufman and Moss Hart
PHOTOGRAPHY Tony Gaudio
EDITOR Jack Killifer
CAST Bette Davis, Ann Sheridan, Monty Woolley, Richard Travis, Jimmy Durante, Reginald Gardiner, Billie Burke, Elizabeth Fraser, Grant Mitchell, George Barbier, Mary Wickes, Russell Arms, Ruth Vivian, Edwin Stanley, Charles Drake, Nanette Vallon, John Ridgely
RUNNING TIME 112 minutes
RELEASED 1 January 1942
PRODUCED BY Warner Bros

48 In This Our Life △
DIRECTOR John Huston
SCENARIO Howard Koch, based on the Pulitzer Prize novel of the same name by Ellen Glasgow
PHOTOGRAPHY Ernest Haller
EDITOR William Holmes
CAST Bette Davis, Olivia de Havilland, George Brent, Dennis Morgan, Charles Coburn, Frank Craven, Billie Burke, Hattie McDaniel, Lee Patrick, Mary Servoss, Ernest Anderson, William B Davison, Edward Fielding, John Hamilton, William Forest, Lee Phelps
RUNNING TIME 97 minutes
RELEASED 8 May 1942
PRODUCED BY Warner Bros

49 Now, Voyager △
DIRECTOR Irving Rapper
SCENARIO Casey Robinson, based on the novel of the same name by Olive Higgins Prouty
PHOTOGRAPHY Sol Polito
EDITOR Warren Low
CAST Bette Davis, Paul Henreid, Claude Rains, Gladys Cooper, Bonita Granville, Ilka Chase, John Loder, Lee Patrick, Franklin Pangborn, Katherine Alexander, James Rennie, Mary Wickes, Janis Wilson, Frank Puglia, Michael Ames, Charles Drake, David Clyde

RUNNING TIME 118 minutes
RELEASED 22 October 1942
PRODUCED BY Warner Bros

50 Watch On The Rhine △
DIRECTOR Herman Shumlin
SCENARIO Dashiell Hammett, with additional scenes and dialogue by Lilian Hellman, based on her play of the same name
PHOTOGRAPHY Merritt Gerstad and Hal Mohr
EDITOR Rudi Fehr
CAST Bette Davis, Paul Lukas, Geraldine Fitzgerald, Lucile Watson, Beulah Bondi, George Coulouris, Donald Woods, Henry Daniell, Donald Buka, Eric Roberts, Janis Wilson, Mary Young, Kurt Katch, Erwin Kalsr, Clyde Fillmore, Robert O Davis, Frank Wilson, Clarence Muse, Anthony Caruso, Howard Hickman, Elvira Curci, Creighton Hale, Alan Hale Jr
RUNNING TIME 115 minutes
RELEASED 27 August 1943
PRODUCED BY Warner Bros

51 Thank Your Lucky Stars △
DIRECTOR David Butler
SCENARIO Norman Panama, Melvin Frank and James V Kern, based on a story by Everett Freeman and Arthur Schwartz
PHOTOGRAPHY Arthur Edeson
EDITOR Irene Morra
CAST Dennis Morgan, Joan Leslie, Edward Everett Horton, S Z Sakall, Richard Lane, Ruth Donnelly, Don Wilson, Henry Armetta, Joyce Reynolds – with guest stars Humphrey Bogart, Eddie Cantor, Bette Davis, Olivia de Havilland, Errol Flynn, John Garfield, Ida Lupino, Ann Sheridan, Dinah Shore, Alexis Smith, Jack Carson, Alan Hale, George Tobias, Hattie McDaniel, Willie Best, Spike Jones and His City Slickers
RUNNING TIME 124 minutes
RELEASED 1 October 1943
PRODUCED BY Warner Bros

52 Old Acquaintance △
DIRECTOR Vincent Sherman
SCENARIO John Van Druten and Lenore
Coffee, based on the play of the same name
by John Van Druten
PHOTOGRAPHY Sol Polito
EDITOR Terry Morse
CAST Bette Davis, Miriam Hopkins, Gig
Young, John Loder, Dolores Moran, Philip
Reed, Roscoe Karns, Anne Revere, Esther
Dale, Ann Codee, Joseph Crehan, Pierre
Watkin, Marjorie Hoshelle, George Lessey,
Ann Doran, Leona Maricle, Francine Rufo
RUNNING TIME 110 minutes
RELEASED 2 November 1943
PRODUCED BY Warner Bros

53 Mr Skeffington △
DIRECTOR Vincent Sherman
SCENARIO Julius J and Philip G Epstein,
based on the novel of the same name by
"Elizabeth"
PHOTOGRAPHY Ernest Haller
EDITOR Ralph Dawson
CAST Bette Davis, Claude Rains, Walter
Abel, Richard Waring, George Coulouris,
Marjorie Riordan, Robert Shayne, John
Alexander, Jerome Cowan, Johnny
Mitchell, Dorothy Peterson, Peter Whitney,
Bill Kennedy, Tom Stevenson, Halliwell
Hobbes, Bunny Sunshine, Gigi Perreau,
Dolores Gray, Walter Kingsford, Molly
Lamont
RUNNING TIME 145 minutes
RELEASED 25 May 1944
PRODUCED BY Warner Bros

54 Hollywood Canteen ▽
DIRECTOR Delmer Daves
SCENARIO Delmer Daves
PHOTOGRAPHY Bert Glennon
EDITOR Christian Nyby
CAST Joan Leslie, Robert Hutton, Janis
Paige, Dane Clark, Richard Erdman, James
Flavin, Joan Winfield, Jonathan Hale,
Rudolph Friml Jr, Bill Manning, Larry

Thompson, Mell Schubert, Walden Boyle,
Steve Richards – with guest stars the
Andrews Sisters, Jack Benny, Joe E Brown,
Eddie Cantor, Kitty Carlisle, Jack Carson,
Joan Crawford, Helmut Dantine, Bette
Davis, Faye Emerson, Victor Francen, John
Garfield, Sydney Greenstreet, Alan Hale,
Paul Henreid, Andrea King, Peter Lorre,
Ida Lupino, Irene Manning, Nora Martin,
Joan McCracken, Dolores Moran, Dennis
Morgan, Eleanor Parker, William Prince,
Joyce Reynolds, John Ridgely, Roy Rogers
and Trigger, S Z Sakall, Alexis Smith,
Zachary Scott, Barbara Stanwyck, Craig
Stevens, Joseph Szigeti, Donald Woods,
Jane Wyman, Jimmy Dorsey and His Band,
Carmen Cavallaro and His Orchestra,
Rosario and Antonio, Sons of the Pioneers,
Virginia Patton, Lynne Baggett, Betty
Alexander, Julie Bishop, Robert Shayne,
Johnny Mitchell, John Sheridan, Colleen
Townsend, Angela Green, Paul Brooke,
Marianne O'Brien, Dorothy Malone, Bill
Kennedy
RUNNING TIME 124 minutes
RELEASED 15 December 1944
PRODUCED BY Warner Bros

55 The Corn Is Green △
DIRECTOR Irving Rapper
SCENARIO Casey Robinson and Frank
Cavett, based on the play of the same name
by Emlyn Williams
PHOTOGRAPHY Sol Polito
EDITOR Frederick Richards
CAST Bette Davis, John Dall, Joan Lorring,
Nigel Bruce, Rhys Williams, Rosalind Ivan,
Mildred Dunnock, Gwenyth Hughes, Billy
Roy, Thomas Louden, Arthur Shields,
Leslie Vincent, Robert Regent, Tony Ellis,
Elliot Dare, Robert Cherry, Gene Ross
RUNNING TIME 115 minutes
RELEASED 29 March 1945
PRODUCED BY Warner Bros

56 A Stolen Life △
DIRECTOR Curtis Bernhardt
SCENARIO Catherine Turney, adapted by
Margaret Buell Wilder, based on the novel
by Karel J Benes, *Uloupeny Zivot*
PHOTOGRAPHY Sol Polito and Ernest Haller
EDITOR Rudi Fehr
CAST Bette Davis, Glenn Ford, Dane Clark,
Walter Brennan, Charles Ruggles, Bruce
Bennett, Peggy Knudsen, Esther Dale,
Clara Blandick, Joan Winfield
RUNNING TIME 109 minutes
RELEASED 1 May 1946
PRODUCED BY Warner Bros, A.B.D.
Productions

57 Deception △
DIRECTOR Irving Rapper
SCENARIO John Collier and Joseph Than,
based on a play variously titled *Monsieur
Lambertheir*, *Satan* and *Jealousy* by Louis
Verneuil
PHOTOGRAPHY Ernest Haller
EDITOR Alan Crosland Jr
CAST Bette Davis, Paul Henreid, Claude
Rains, John Abbott, Benson Fong, Richard
Walsh, Suzi Crandall, Richard Erdman,
Ross Ford, Russell Arms, Bess Flowers,
Gino Cerrado, Clifton Young, Cyril
Delevanti, Jane Harker
RUNNING TIME 110 minutes
RELEASED 18 October 1946
PRODUCED BY Warner Bros

58 Winter Meeting ▽
DIRECTOR Bretaigne Windust
SCENARIO Catherine Turney, based on the
novel of the same name by Ethel Vance
PHOTOGRAPHY Ernest Haller
EDITOR Owen Marks
CAST Bette Davis, Janis Paige, James Davis,
John Hoyt, Florence Bates, Walter
Baldwin, Ransom Sherman

RUNNING TIME 104 minutes
RELEASED 7 April 1948
PRODUCED BY Warner Bros

59 June Bride △
DIRECTOR Bretaigne Windust
SCENARIO Ranald McDougall, based on the
play *Feature for June* by Eileen Tighe and
Graeme Lorimer
PHOTOGRAPHY Ted McCord
EDITOR Owen Marks
CAST Bette Davis, Robert Montgomery, Fay
Bainter, Betty Lynn, Tom Tully, Barbara
Bates, Jerome Cowan, Mary Wickes, James
Burke, Raymond Roe, Marjorie Bennett,
Ray Montgomery, George O'Hanlon,
Sandra Gould, Esther Howard, Jessie
Adams, Raymond Bond, Alice Kelley,
Patricia Northrop
RUNNING TIME 96 minutes
RELEASED 29 October 1948
PRODUCED BY Warner Bros

60 Beyond the Forest ▽
DIRECTOR King Vidor
SCENARIO Lenore Coffee, based on the novel
of the same name by Stuart Engstrand

PHOTOGRAPHY Robert Burks
EDITOR Rudi Fehr
CAST Bette Davis, Joseph Cotten, David
Brian, Ruth Roman, Minor Watson, Dona
Drake, Regis Toomey, Sarah Selby, Mary
Servoss, Frances Charles, Harry Tyler,
Ralph Littlefield, Creighton Hale, Joel
Allen, Ann Doran
RUNNING TIME 97 minutes
RELEASED 21 October 1949
PRODUCED BY Warner Bros

61 All About Eve △
DIRECTOR Joseph Mankiewicz
SCENARIO Joseph Mankiewicz, based on the
story *The Wisdom of Eve* by Mary Orr
PHOTOGRAPHY Milton Krasner
EDITOR Barbara McLean
CAST Bette Davis, Anne Baxter, George
Sanders, Celeste Holm, Gary Merrill, Hugh
Marlowe, Thelma Ritter, Marilyn Monroe,
Gregory Ratoff, Barbara Bates, Walter
Hampden, Randy Stuart, Craig Hill, Leland
Harris, Claude Stroud, Eugene Borden,
Steve Geray, Bess Flowers, Stanley Orr,
Eddie Fisher
RUNNING TIME 138 minutes
RELEASED 13 October 1950
PRODUCED BY Twentieth Century-Fox

62 Payment On Demand △
DIRECTOR Curtis Bernhardt
PHOTOGRAPHY Leo Tover
EDITOR Harry Marker
CAST Bette Davis, Barry Sullivan, Jane
Cowl, Kent Taylor, Betty Lynn, John
Sutton, Frances Dee, Peggie Castle, Otto
Kruger, Walter Sande, Brett King, Richard
Anderson, Natalie Schafer, Katherine
Emery, Lisa Golm, Moroni Olsen
RUNNING TIME 91 minutes
RELEASED 15 February 1951
PRODUCED BY RKO Radio

63 Another Man's Poison ▽
DIRECTOR Irving Rapper
SCENARIO Val Guest, based on the play

Deadlock by Leslie Sands
PHOTOGRAPHY Robert Krasker
EDITOR Gordon Hales
CAST Bette Davis, Gary Merrill, Emlyn
Williams, Anthony Steel, Barbara Murray,
Reginald Beckwith, Edna Morris
RUNNING TIME 88 minutes
RELEASED 6 January 1952
PRODUCED BY Eros Productions, released by
United Artists

64 Phone Call From A Stranger △
DIRECTOR Jean Negulesco
SCENARIO Nunnally Johnson, based on a
story by Ida Alexa Ross Wylie
PHOTOGRAPHY Milton Krasner
EDITOR Hugh Fowler
CAST Shelley Winters, Gary Merrill,
Michael Rennie, Keenan Wynn, Evelyn
Varden, Warren Stevens, Beatrice Straight,
Ted Donaldson, Craig Stevens, Helen
Westcott, Bette Davis
RUNNING TIME 90 minutes
RELEASED 1 February 1952
PRODUCED BY Twentieth Century-Fox

65 The Star △
DIRECTOR Stuart Heisler
SCENARIO and original story by Katherine
Albert and Dale Eunson
PHOTOGRAPHY Ernest Laszlo
EDITOR Otto Ludwig

CAST Bette Davis, Sterling Hayden, Natalie Wood, Warner Anderson, Minor Watson, June Travis, Katherine Warren, Kay Riehl, Barbara Woodel, Fay Baker, Barbara Lawrence, David Alpert, Paul Frees
RUNNING TIME 90 minutes
RELEASED 28 January 1953
PRODUCED BY Bert E Friedlob Productions, released by Twentieth Century-Fox

66 The Virgin Queen △
DIRECTOR Henry Koster
SCENARIO and original story *Sir Walter Raliegh* by Harry Brown and Mindred Lord
PHOTOGRAPHY Charles G Clarke
EDITOR Robert Simpson
CAST Bette Davis, Richard Todd, Joan Collins, Joy Robinson, Herbert Marshall, Dan O'Herlihy, Robert Douglas, Romney Brent, Marjorie Hellen, Lisa Daniels, Lisa Davis, Barry Bernard, Robert Adler, Noel Drayton, Ian Murray, Margery Weston, Rod Taylor, Davis Thursby, Arthur Gould-Porter
RUNNING TIME 92 minutes
RELEASED 5 August 1955
PRODUCED BY Twentieth Century-Fox

67 The Catered Affair △
DIRECTOR Richard Brooks
SCENARIO Gore Vidal, based on the teleplay of the same name by Paddy Chayefsky
PHOTOGRAPHY John Alton
EDITOR Gene Ruggiero and Frank Santillo
CAST Bette Davis, Debbie Reynolds, Ernest Borgnine, Barry Fitzgerald, Rod Taylor, Robert Simon, Madge Kennedy, Dorothy Stickney, Carol Veazie, Joan Camden, Ray Stricklyn, Jay Adler, Dan Tobin, Paul Denton, Augusta Merighi, Sammy Shack, Jack Kenny, Robert Stephenson, Mae Clarke
RUNNING TIME 92 minutes
RELEASED 14 June 1956
PRODUCED BY Metro-Goldwyn-Mayer

68 Storm Centre △
DIRECTOR Daniel Taradash
SCENARIO Daniel Taradash and Elick Moll
PHOTOGRAPHY Burnett Guffey
EDITOR William A Lyon
CAST Bette Davis, Brian Keith, Kim Hunter, Paul Kelly, Kevin Coughlin, Joe Mantell, Sallie Brophy, Howard Wierum, Curtis Cooksey, Michael Raffetto, Edward Platt, Kathryn Grant, Howard Wendell, Burt Mustin, Edith Evanson
RUNNING TIME 86 minutes
RELEASED 20 October 1956
PRODUCED BY Phoenix Productions, released by Columbia Pictures

69 John Paul Jones △
DIRECTOR John Farrow
SCENARIO John Farrow and Jesse Lasky Jr, from the story *Nor'wester* by Clements Ripley
PHOTOGRAPHY Michel Kelber
EDITOR Eda Warren
CAST Robert Stack, Marisa Pavan, Charles Coburn, Erin O'Brien, Tom Brannum, Bruce Cabot, Basil Sydney, Archie Duncan, Thomas Gomex, Judson Laure, Bob Cunningham, John Charles Farrow, Eric Pohlmann, Pepe Nieto, John Crawford, Patrick Villiers, Frank Latimore, Ford Rainey, Bruce Seaton, MacDonald Carey, Jean Pierre Aumont, David Farrar, Peter Cushing, Susana Canales, Jorge Riviere and Bette Davis as Catherine the Great
RUNNING TIME 126 minutes
RELEASED 16 June 1959
PRODUCED BY Samuel Bronston Productions

70 The Scapegoat ▽
DIRECTOR Robert Hamer
SCENARIO Gore Vidal and Robert Hamer, based on the novel of the same name by Daphne du Maurier
PHOTOGRAPHY Paul Beeson
EDITOR Jack Harris
CAST Alec Guinness, Bette Davis, Nicole Maurey, Irene Worth, Pamela Brown,

Annabel Bartlett, Geoffrey Keen, Noel Howlett, Peter Bull, Leslie French, Alan Webb, Maria Britneva, Eddie Byrne, Alexander Archdale, Peter Sallis
RUNNING TIME 92 minutes
RELEASED 6 August 1959
PRODUCED BY Maurier-Guinness Productions, released by Metro-Goldwyn-Mayer

71 Pocketful Of Miracles △
DIRECTOR Frank Capra
SCENARIO Hal Kanter and Harry Tugend, based on the screenplay *Lady for a Day* by Robert Riskin and the *Madame la Gimp* by Damon Runyon
PHOTOGRAPHY Robert Bronner
EDITOR Frank P Keller
CAST Glenn Ford, Bette Davis, Hope Lange, Arthur O'Connell, Peter Falk, Thomas Mitchell, Edward Everett Horton, Mickey Shaughnessy, David Brian, Sheldon Leonard, Ann-Margret, Peter Mann, Barton MacLane, John Litel, Jerome Cowan, Jay Novello, Frank Ferguson, Willis Bouchey, Fritz Feld, Ellen Corby, Gavin Gordon, Benny Rubin, Jack Elam, Mike Mazurki, Hayden Rorke, Doodles Weaver, Paul E Burns, George E Stone, Snub Pollard
RUNNING TIME 136 minutes
RELEASED 18 December 1961
PRODUCED BY Franton Productions, released by United Artists

72 Whatever Happened to Baby Jane? ▷
DIRECTOR Robert Aldrich
SCENARIO Lukas Heller, based on the novel of the same name by Henry Farrell
PHOTOGRAPHY Ernest Haller
CAST Bette Davis, Joan Crawford, Victor Buono, Marjorie Bennett, Maidie Norman, Anne Lee, Barbara Merrill, Julie Aldred, Gina Gillespie, Dave Willock, Ann Barton
RUNNING TIME 132 minutes

RELEASED 6 November 1962
PRODUCED BY Seven Arts Associates and Aldrich Productions, released by Warner Bros

73 Dead Ringer △

DIRECTOR Paul Henreid
SCENARIO Albert Beich and Oscar Millard, based on the story *La Otra* or *Dead Pigeon* by Rian James
PHOTOGRAPHY Ernest Haller
EDITOR Folmar Blangsted
CAST Bette Davis, Karl Malden, Peter Lawford, Philip Carey, Jean Hagen, George Macready, Estelle Winwood, George Chandler, Mario Alcade, Cyril Delevanti, Monika Henreid, Bert Remsen, Charles Watts, Ken Lynch
RUNNING TIME 115 minutes
RELEASED 19 February 1964
PRODUCED BY Warner Bros

74 The Empty Canvas △

DIRECTOR Damiano Damiani
SCENARIO Tonino Guerra, Ugo Liberatore and Damiano Damiani, based on the novel *La Noia (Bordom)* by Alberto Moravia
PHOTOGRAPHY Roberto Gerardi
EDITOR Renzo Lucidi
CAST Bette Davis, Horst Buchholz, Catherine Spaak, Daniela Rocca, Lea Padovani, Isa Miranda, Leonida Repaci, George Wilson, Marcella Rovena, Daniela Calvino, Renato Moretti, Edorado Nevola,

Jole Mauro, Mario Lanfranchi
RUNNING TIME 118 minutes
RELEASED 15 May 1964
PRODUCED BY Joseph E Levine – Carlo Ponti Production, released by Embassy Pictures

75 Where Love Has Gone △

DIRECTOR Edward Dmytryk
SCENARIO John Michael Hayes, based on the novel of the same name by Harold Robbins
PHOTOGRAPHY Joseph MacDonald
EDITOR Frank Bracht
CAST Susan Hayward, Bette Davies, Michael Connors, Joey Heatherton, Jane Greer, DeForest Kelley, George Macready, Anne Seymour, Willis Bouchey, Walter Reed, Ann Doran, Bartlett Robinson, Whit Bissell, Anthony Caruso, Jack Greening, Olga Sutcliffe, Howard Wendell, Colin Kenny
RUNNING TIME 114 minutes
RELEASED 2 Novemeber 1964
PRODUCED BY Joseph E Levine Production, released by Paramount

76 Hush . . . Hush, Sweet Charlotte △

DIRECTOR Robert Aldrich
SCENARIO Henry Farrell and Lukas Heller, based on a story by Henry Farrell

PHOTOGRAPHY Joseph Biroc
EDITOR Michael Luciano
CAST Bette Davis, Olivia de Havilland, Joseph Cotten, Agnes Moorhead, Cecil Kellaway, Victor Buono, Mary Astor, William Campbell, Wesley Addy, Bruce Dern, George Kennedy, Dave Willock, John Megna, Ellen Corby, Helen Kleeb, Marianne Stewart, Frank Ferguson, Mary Henderson, Lilian Randolph, Geraldine West, William Walker, Idell James, Teddy Buckner and His All-Stars
RUNNING TIME 134 minutes
RELEASED 15 December 1964
PRODUCED BY Associates and Aldrich Production, released by Twentieth Century-Fox

77 The Nanny △

DIRECTOR Seth Holt
SCENARIO Jimmy Sangster, based on the novel of the same name by Evelyn Piper
PHOTOGRAPHY Harry Waxman
EDITOR James Needs
CAST Bette Davis, Wendy Craig, Jill Bennett, James Villiers, William Dix, Pamela Franklin, Jack Watling, Maurice Denham, Alfred Burke, Nora Gordon, Sandra Power, Harry Fowler
RUNNING TIME 93 minutes
RELEASED 3 November 1965
PRODUCED BY Seven Arts-Hammer Films, released by Twentieth Century-Fox

78 The Anniversary △

DIRECTOR Roy Ward Baker
SCENARIO Jimmy Sangster, based on the play of the same name by Bill MacIlwraith
PHOTOGRAPHY Harry Waxman
EDITOR Peter Wetherly
CAST Bette Davis, Sheila Hancock, Jack Hedley, James Cossins, Christian Roberts, Elaine Taylor, Timothy Bateson, Arnold Diamond
RUNNING TIME 95 minutes
RELEASED 20 March 1968
PRODUCED BY Seven Arts-Hammer Production, released by Twentieth Century-Fox

79 Connecting Rooms △
DIRECTOR Franklin Gollings
SCENARIO Franklin Gollings, based on the play of the same name by Marion Hart
CAST Bette Davis, Michael Redgrave, Alexis Kanner, Kay Walsh, Gabrielle Drake, Olga Georges-Picot, Leo Genn, Richard Wyler
RUNNING TIME 103 minutes
RELEASED May 1971
PRODUCED BY LSD Productions

80 Bunny O'Hare △
DIRECTOR Gerd Oswald
SCENARIO Stanley Z Cherry and Coslough Johnson, based on the story *Bunny and Billy* by Stanley Z Cherry
PHOTOGRAPHY Loyal Griggs and John Stephens
EDITOR Fred Feitshans Jr
CAST Bette Davis, Ernest Borgnine, Jack Cassidy, Joan Delaney, Jay Robinson, John Astin, Reva Rose
RUNNING TIME 92 minutes
RELEASED 18 October 1971
PRODUCED BY American International Pictures

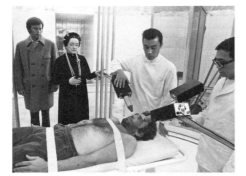

81 Madame Sin* △
DIRECTOR David Greene
SCENARIO Barry Oringer and David Greene, from an original concept by Lou Morheim and Barry Shear
PHOTOGRAPHY Tony Richmond
CAST Bette Davis, Robert Wagner,

Denholm Elliott, Gordon Jackson, Dudley Sutton, Catherine Schell, Paul Maxwell, Piksen Lim
RELEASED 12 May 1972
PRODUCED BY 2X Productions

82 The Judge and Jake Wyler*
DIRECTOR David Lowell Rich
SCENARIO David Shaw, Richard Levinson and William Link
PHOTOGRAPHY William Margulies
EDITOR Bud Small
CAST Bette Davis, Doug McClure, Eric Braeden, Joan Van Ark, Gary Conway, Lou Jacobi, James McEachin, Lizabeth Hush, Kent Smith, Barbara Rhoades
RELEASED NBC Movie of the Week, 2 December 1972
PRODUCED BY Universal Television

83 Lo Scopone Scientifico (The Scientific Cardplayer Or The Game) △
DIRECTOR Luigi Comencini
SCENARIO Rodolfo Sonego
PHOTOGRAPHY Guiseppi Ruzzolini
EDITOR Bruno Cesari
CAST Alberto Sordi, Somvana Mangano, Joseph Cotten, Bette Davis, Domenico Modugno, Mario Carotenuto
RUNNING TIME 118 minutes
RELEASED 16 October 1972
PRODUCED BY CIC Productions

84 Scream, Pretty Peggy*
DIRECTOR Gordon Hessler
SCENARIO Jimmy Sangster and Arthur Hoffe
PHOTOGRAPHY Lennie South
EDITOR Larry Strong
CAST Bette Davis, Ted Bessell, Sean Barbara Allen, Charles Drake
RELEASED NBC Movie of the Week, 22 November 1973
PRODUCED BY Universal Television

85 Burnt Offerings ▽
DIRECTOR Dan Curtis

SCENARIO William F Nolan and Dan Curtis, from Robert Marasco's novel
PHOTOGRAPHY Jacques Marquette
EDITOR Dennis Virkler
CAST Bette Davis, Karen Black, Oliver Reed, Burgess Meredith, Eileen Heckart, Lee Montgomery, Dub Taylor
RUNNING TIME 115 minutes
RELEASED 1976
PRODUCED BY PEA Films in association with Dan Curtis Productions for United Artists

86 The Disappearance of Aimee aka Sister Aimee*
DIRECTOR Anthony Harvey
SCENARIO John McGreevey
PHOTOGRAPHY Jim Crabbe
CAST Bette Davis, Faye Dunaway, James Sloyan, James Woods, Barry Brown, William Jordan, John Lehne, Severn Darden
RUNNING TIME 120 minutes
RELEASED 17 November 1976
PRODUCED BY Tomorrow Entertainment

87 The Dark Secret Of Harvest Home*
DIRECTOR Leo Penn
SCENARIO Jack Guss and Charles E Israel from the novel *Harvest Home* by Thomas Tryon
CAST Bette Davis, David Ackroyd, Joanna Miles, Rene Auberjonois, Norman Lloyd, John Calvin, Donald Pleasance (narrator)
RUNNING TIME 300 minutes
RELEASED 23 and 24 January 1978
PRODUCED BY Universal Television

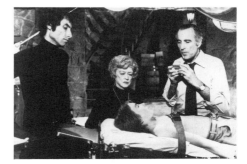

88 Return From Witch Mountain △
DIRECTOR John Hough
SCENARIO Malcolm Marmorstein
PHOTOGRAPHY Frank Phillips
EDITOR Bob Bring
CAST Bette Davis, Christopher Lee, Ike Elsenmann, Jack Soo, Kim Richards, Dick Bakalyan
RUNNING TIME 93 minutes
RELEASED 1978
PRODUCED BY Buena Vista/Walt Disney Productions

89 Death On The Nile ▷
DIRECTOR John Guillermin
SCENARIO Anthony Shaffer from Agatha Christie's novel
PHOTOGRAPHY Jack Cardiff
EDITOR Malcolm Cooke
CAST Bette Davis, Peter Ustinov, Jane Birkin, Lois Chiles, Mia Farrow, Jon Finch, Olivia Hussey, George Kennedy, Angela Lansbury, Simon MacCorkingdale, David

Niven, Maggie Smith, Jack Warden, Harry Andrews, Sam Wanamaker
RUNNING TIME 140 minutes
RELEASED 1978
PRODUCED BY Mersham for EMI

90 Strangers: The Story Of A Mother And Daughter*
DIRECTOR Milton Katselas
SCENARIO Michael de Guzman
CAST Bette Davis, Gena Rowlands, Ford Rainey, Donald Moffat, Whit Bissell, Royal Dano, Kate Riehl
RELEASED 13 May 1979
PRODUCED BY Chris-Rose Productions

91 Watcher In The Woods △
DIRECTOR John Hough
SCENARIO Brian Clemens, Rosemary Anne Sisson and Gerry Day
PHOTOGRAPHY Alan Hume
EDITOR Geoffrey Foot
CAST Bette Davis, David McCallum, Carroll Baker, Ian Bannen, Richard Pasco, Frances Cuka, Lynn-Holly Johnson, Kyle Richards
RUNNING TIME 100 minutes
RELEASED 1980
PRODUCED BY Buena Vista (Walt Disney Productions)

92 White Mama*
DIRECTOR Jackie Cooper
SCENARIO Robert C S Downs
CAST Bette Davis, Ernest Harden Jr, Eileen Heckart, Virginia Capers, Anne Ramsey, Lurene Tuttle
RUNNING TIME 120 minutes
RELEASED 5 March 1980
PRODUCED BY Tomorrow Entertainment

93 Skyward*
DIRECTOR Ron Howard
CAST Bette Davis
RELEASED 20 November 1980
PRODUCED BY NBC Television/General Electric

94 Family Reunion*
DIRECTOR Fielder Cook
CAST Bette Davis, J Ashley Hyman
RUNNING TIME 240 minutes
RELEASED 11 and 12 October 1981
PRODUCED BY Creative Projects Inc in association with Columbia Pictures Television

95 Right of Way*
DIRECTOR George Schaefer
SCENARIO Richard Lees
PHOTOGRAPHY Howard Schwartz
EDITOR Sid Katz
CAST Bette Davis, Jimmy Stewart, Melinda Dillon, Priscilla Morrill, John Harkins, Louis Schaefer, Jacque Lynn Colton
RELEASED 1983
PRODUCED BY Schaefer/Karpf Productions/ Post Newsweek Video for HBO (Home Box Office)
* = television movie

STAGEWORK
1928

The Famous Mrs Fare (Spring, Provincetown Playhouse, Greenwich Village, New York)
DIRECTOR James Light, for the John Murray Anderson School

The Charm School (Summer)
The Junior Players, East Dennis, Mass.

Mr Pim Passes By (Summer)
The Cape Playhouse, Dennis, Mass.

The Silver Chord (Summer)
The Cape Playhouse, Dennis, Mass.

Stock: Davis acted in *Excess Baggage* with Miriam Hopkins, *Yellow* with Louis Calhern, and *The Squall* and *Broadway* and other plays for the George Cukor-George Kondolf Stock Company at the Temple Theatre, Rochester, NY for the fall season.

The Earth Between (Winter, Provincetown Playhouse, New York)
by Virgil Geddes
CAST William Challee, Bette Davis, Carroll Ashburn, Janne Burbie, Warren Colston
PRODUCED BY James Light and M Eleanor Fitzgerald

1929

Stock: *The Constant Wife, The Patsy* and *You Can Never Tell* at the Cape Playhouse, Dennis, Mass. for the summer season. Davis portrayed Hedvig in *The Wild Duck* and also appeared in *The Lady from the Sea*, both by Ibsen, for the Blanche Yurka Company on tour for the fall season.

Broken Dishes (November, Ritz Theatre, New York, and afterwards on tour)
by Martin Flavin
DIRECTOR/PRODUCER Marion Gering
CAST Donald Meek, Bette Davis, Ellen F

Lowe, Etha Dack, Eda Heineman, Reed Brown, J Francis-Robertson, Duncan Penwarden, Josef Lazarovici

1930

Stock: Davis played the role of Dinah in *Mr Pim* for the Cape Players, Dennis, Mass. for the spring season.

Solid South (October, Lyceum Theatre, New York)
by Lawton Campbell
CAST Richard Bennett, Elizabeth Patterson, Jessie Royce Landis, Georgette Harvey, Owen Davis Jr, Richard Huey, Moffat Johnson, Lew Payton
PRODUCED BY Alexander McKaig

1952

Two's Company (October, Shubert Theatre, Detroit, Mich., thereafter at Nixon Theatre, Pittsburgh, Pa. and Shubert Theatre, Boston Mass; December, Alvin Theatre, New York)
by Charles Sherman
DIRECTOR Jules Dassin
MUSIC Vernon Duke, Genevive Pitot, David Baker
CAST Bette Davis, Hiram Sherman, Nora Kaye, Bill Callahan, Stanley Praeger, George Irving, Pete Kelley, Maria Karnilova, Ann Hathaway, Nathaniel Frey, Robert Orton's Teen Aces, plus singers and dancers
PRESENTED BY James Russo and Michael Ellis

1959

The World of Carl Sandburg (October, State Theatre, Portland, Me. and afterwards on tour)
adapted from the works of Carl Sandburg
DIRECTOR Norman Corwin
CAST Bette Davis and Gary Merrill, with guitarist-balladeer Clark Allen
PRESENTED BY Armand Deutsch, in association with Judd Bernard

1961

The night of the Iguana (November, Blackstone Theatre, Chicago, Ill.; December, Royale Theatre, New York)
by Tennessee Williams
DIRECTOR Frank Corsaro
CAST Bette Davis, Margaret Leighton, Alan Webb, Patrick O'Neal, Patricia Rose, Christopher Jones, James Farentino, Bruce Glover, Laryssa Lauret, Heinz Hohenwald, Lucy Landau, Theseus George, Lane Bradbury, Louis Guss
PRESENTED BY Charles Bowden

1974

Miss Moffat (Autumn, Broadway)
A musical version of *The Corn is Green* by Emlyn Williams
DIRECTOR Josh Logan